Prair

"Cathleen's st .... nspiration and emp .... ulnerability. It's about how we keep moving forward through our heartache and pain, and how we learn to love ourselves in the darkness. In Shattered Together, Cathleen shows us that not only do we have the power to endure any and all losses, but we have the ability to come out on the other side of them stronger, more loving, more compassionate, and more forgiving."

—**Jack Canfield,** Coauthor of the bestselling *Chicken Soup for the Soul®* series and *The Success Principles™: How to Get from Where You Are to Where You Want to Be*

"*Shattered Together* is a powerfully honest book. Cathleen Elle's willingness to share her raw and intimate times following the loss of her son carries you along with her into healing. If you have experienced the death of a loved one or you work with people who have, I highly recommend this book."

—**Deborah Sandella** PhD, RN, originator of the *Regenerating Images in Memory Method (RIM)* and #1 International Bestselling author of *Goodbye Hurt & Pain, 7 Simple Steps to Health, Love and Success*

"Cathleen Elle is a rare and gifted truth-teller. Her story is raw, yet real, unfiltered, and so is the inspiration. She shines a light on her journey to illuminate ours, and to show us that no matter our grief, we can still find our way to the light."

—**Kate Butler,** Certified Professional Success Coach, International Speaker, and #1 Bestselling Author of *Women Who Rise: 30 Stories That Inspire Your Spirit To Rise!*

"Cathleen Elle's moving story teaches us that no matter how painful our loss, there is hope, there is healing, there is a life to still be lived, and love to still be experienced - Cathleen is living proof."

—**Patty Aubrey,** President of The Canfield Training Group and past president of Chicken Soup for the Soul Ent, Inc. and founder of the Permission Granted project

"A masterpiece of emotional processing. Cathleen's beautiful healing journey will touch you, inspire you, move you, and help you heal. Her willingness to be vulnerable is a true gift to the reader. As I unwrapped the gift, I cried with sadness, I cried with joy, I cried with love. I learned so much about loss and recovery and I learned things I didn't know about my own losses large and small. Take a gentle step into Shattered Together in whatever way feels right to you and, as incongruent with grief as it sounds, enjoy."

— **Michael J. Kline,** Senior Trainer, The RIM Institute and founder of Intus, Personal and Group Transformation

Kim —

Spending time with you has been a true honor!
I look forward to continuing to connect + see all you consciously create!,

With Love + Light
Cathleen Elle

Shattered Together

First Edition

Copyright ©2020 Cathleen Elle

All rights reserved.

ISBN: 978-1-952725-18-0

Disclaimer: The author of this book does not dispense medical advice or prescribe the use of any technique as a form of treatment for physical, emotional, or medical problems without the advice of a physician, either directly or indirectly. The intent of the author is only to offer information of a general nature to help you in your quest for emotional, physical, and spiritual well-being. In the event you use any of the information in this book for yourself, the authors and the publisher assume no responsibility for your actions.

Cover Design by Bumi Benjamin

Interior formatting by Melissa Williams Design

www.katebutlerbooks.com

Contents

Shattered Together

A MOTHER'S JOURNEY FROM GRIEF TO BELIEF

A Guide to Help You Through Sudden Loss

CATHLEEN ELLE

To my daughter, Ashley, for giving me reason to continue living when I didn't think I could.

To my son, Logan, for sending messages from above that kept me going on this journey when I didn't think I could take another step.

Foreword

By Jack Canfield

When we rise up and have the courage to tell our stories, not only do we heal, we can heal others too.

As the co-author of the bestselling *Chicken Soup for the Soul*® series, and as the author or co-author of more than 170 books (47 of which are *New York Times* bestsellers), I've seen this magic work again and again.

Which brings me to Cathleen. We met during a day-long workshop I hosted in Boston. We sat next to each other at lunch, and I remember being struck by her positivity. She radiated joy and put all of our lunch-mates at ease.

When she told me she was a healer who helped people work through trauma, grief, and sudden loss, I thought *those are intense subjects for someone who seems so light and happy*. But then I asked her what had inspired her to go into the healing arts.

"My son," she said. I could hear the strength and determination in her voice and also a little quiver of emotion. I encouraged her to go on and she told me about how she felt her life had shattered when her 19-year-old son, Logan, had died by suicide. She told me how hard she had worked to pick up the pieces over the last eight years, how painful and dark those first few years were, and how she wasn't sure if she deserved to go on living. But slowly, as she invested in her healing, she began to move through the darkness and she could feel the light once more.

"Everyone deserves to heal and to feel loved," she said to me.

I knew right then how important Cathleen's story and journey would be. She would go on to take my Train the Trainer program where I had the opportunity to get to know her for the extraordinary woman, mother, friend, and healer that she is.

She knows how to help people heal through their pain, because she's done it for herself. She knows sudden unexpected loss. She knows what happens when someone or something vitally important in our lives gets torn from us. And she knows what it's like to have our lives shattered instantly, and what it takes to gather those pieces again to create a new life and self—born not from pain, but from love and faith and forgiveness.

I can't think of a more important story and message for the world to receive right now.

Sudden and unexpected loss surrounds many of us. We lose loved ones, our health and vitality, our jobs and livelihoods, our normal routines, our friends, our financial security, and our dreams. Our lives and the world that we had come to know, often vanishes.

We realize there is no going back to life as we had known it. That's a tough idea to embrace. Thankfully, Cathleen knows a way forward and has shown us a path through our losses and our grief in *Shattered Together*.

This is our guidebook into a new, uncertain, unchartered world. Not only does Cathleen share the story of how her life and self was shattered after her son's death, she also shows us how she pieced her life and self, back together. She gives us the teachings and lessons she learned along the way while offering us actionable practices that we can weave into our daily lives, right now.

Cathleen's story is about resiliency and perseverance, inspiration and empowerment, courage and vulnerability. It's about how we keep moving forward through our heartache and pain, and how we learn to love ourselves in the darkness. In *Shattered Together*, Cathleen shows us that not only do we have the power to endure any and all losses, but we have the ability to come out on the other side of them stronger, more loving, more compassionate, and more forgiving.

I know that Cathleen's story will inspire you. I hope that as you read and absorb her messages, that you realize how important your story is too.

May you find healing and a way forward in this brave new world.

—Jack Canfield

Coauthor of the bestselling *Chicken Soup for the Soul®* series and *The Success Principles™: How to Get from Where You Are to Where You Want to Be*

Introduction

On March 31, 2010, my nineteen-year-old son, Logan, died by suicide and my life, the person I was, and the future I had always imagined were instantly shattered.

What do you do when you lose a loved one suddenly and unexpectedly? How do you go on living? Is that even possible? Who do you become? What do you do with your life? What does your life look like?

For many years I didn't know how to answer these questions and honestly, I wasn't even capable of doing so. When Logan took his life, he wasn't speaking with me and left a note saying he didn't want me to attend his service. I was devastated.

In fact, the last two years of Logan's life had been difficult for us. He battled with mental health issues that most people didn't know about. In spite of receiving care from different doctors, we were not able to find a treatment that was successful for him.

Our relationship suffered as I did my best to set boundaries while also trying to help him. Over those last two years I had struggled to reach my son. After our last fight, Logan stormed out of our home and hadn't spoken with me for a few weeks. I figured this latest silence was a phase and eventually he would respond to my texts and calls. I thought with some time and distance, we'd find our way back together. *It is just a speed bump*, I told myself.

But I was wrong. Suicide would take my son's life and forever alter mine and everyone's around him.

Understanding Death as a Transition

Throughout this book, you will see that I refer to death as a transition. I believe, at our core, we are all energy. Energy cannot be made. It cannot die. It can only be transformed. When we die, I believe our energy becomes free from our physical forms (i.e. our bodies) and transforms into spirit. As such, our loved one's energy is always with us and it's always around us.

To say my world, my heart, and my soul were shattered is an understatement. Logan's transition broke me. I was left bearing so much blame, shame, and guilt that I didn't know how I would ever go on living. There was a time where I truly wasn't sure I could. The grief was so overwhelming that it hurt just breathing. Memories of all my screw ups, what I should have said, what I should have done, and what I should have been able to prevent, haunted me.

I was someone who "had it all together." I was a business owner. I served for eight years in the Vermont House of Representatives where I sat on powerful committees including House Appropriations and House Judiciary. We had debated and passed the groundbreaking Civil Unions bill, the first in the country. I had an appointed position in the Governor's administration. At the time of Logan's transition, I was leading a multi-million-dollar trade association, one of the most influential in the state.

How had I let my son's transition happen? I could barely face people in my community let alone the face that stared back at me in the mirror. And yet, ten years later, here I am working as a transformational speaker, an intuitive coach, and a healer.

What changed? How did I go from the overwhelming self-hatred, blame, and guilt to a place where I help other people who have lost someone suddenly and unexpectedly? In this book, I will share with you how I came to realized I had two choices: I could live a life filled with pain, walking through the world in a fog of grief, *or* I could invest in myself and go on a healing journey. I chose the healing journey.

I am someone who believes there is a reason and purpose for our lives and that we can grow from everything that we endure and experience. I vowed to myself and my son that I would take our tragedy and use it to help other people learn how to pick up and put together the pieces of their shattered lives and selves. I vowed to find a way to move from the darkness into the light.

For the last decade, this has been my journey: from darkness to light, grief to love, shame to pride, guilt to forgiveness. As I worked to move through my grief, the further along on my healing journey I went my life slowly changed. People would ask me what I had done, what was I doing, and how they too could heal. I started sharing my story publicly in interviews on television, radio, and in print. I posted on social media and I gave public speeches at high schools, businesses, organizations, and at conferences, speaking about suicide prevention and how to heal after a loss. I began hearing from people, thanking me for giving voice to their experiences, for giving them hope, and for helping them to transform their lives too.

Now, in the coming pages I will share my story with

you. I will give to you some of the most significant moments on my intense healing journey, the mindsets I've had to adopt, the lessons I've had to learn, and the practices and tools that I use that have helped me redesign my life, both internally and externally, in a way that honors my son and my Self.

I share my healing journey and what has worked for me in the hopes that you too may find healing, guidance, and support on your path.

I've divided the book into two parts. In Part One, I debunk some of society's most harmful myths surrounding the sudden and unexpected loss of a loved one. These are the "truths" (as I have come to know them, and as many other people I have coached and spoken with have experienced them) that I wish someone had shared with me. These messages form the foundation for our healing journeys, and they can be revisited as often as necessary. I use them as mantras when I feel myself slipping into the darkness (yes, that still happens occasionally, but it never lasts as long and it's not as intense).

In Part Two, I share some of the major milestones and turning points on my healing journey, the lessons I've learned, and how I've applied them in my life. Each chapter includes a *Daily Practice* that I've used and found especially helpful as I've moved through that particular experience. I will walk you through how to incorporate the practice into your life, if you wish to try them. I don't expect you to add every practice into your life at once—actually, please don't! That would be too much to shoulder. Instead, try picking one chapter and practice what strongly resonates with you. Try adding that practice into your daily life for one week and see how you feel. You can incorporate more practices over time.

Each chapter is designed to build on the next, covering

the major milestones and awakenings I've had on this journey. However, if there's one lesson that I continue receiving, it's that we are not on a linear journey. I have circled back to many of these milestones over the last ten years. While I recommend this book be read from start to finish, skipping around works too. So, if you find a chapter calls to you, then go to it. The choice is yours and there is no right or wrong way to read this book, just as there is no right or wrong way for you to make your way through your healing journey.

This book is meant to help jumpstart your healing journey, but it is in no way a complete guide, miracle cure, or a replacement for other support that may be available to you. I'll mention this a few times throughout the book, but I encourage you to *please seek professional guidance* (if you aren't already). I owe a great deal of appreciation to the many healers, spiritual leaders, counselors, therapists, intuitives, mentors, coaches, and mediums who have helped me throughout the years. You are not meant to walk this alone. There are people out there waiting to help you.

Some chapters and the practices may resonate very strongly with you today, while others may not. If you read this book a month or a year from now, you may find yourself pulled toward different chapters. This is okay. Embrace whatever arises and continue on your journey.

I have intentionally offered some very raw stories and the emotions I had experienced. I value transparency and honesty, and I don't want to sugar-coat anything. However, I recognize that, for some people, these stories may be very difficult to read. If you find yourself having a strong reaction to any story or chapter and it's too difficult for you, then skip it. You are in control of this journey, please remember that. I trust that you know what you need, and when you need it.

Above all, please be kind to yourself and do what's right for you, always. Everything in this book is *my* journey and experiences. It may not be exactly like yours. You may experience other milestones or have a different interpretation of a similar one. All of that is okay. Use whatever you can from my story and take whatever practices make sense for you. I offer everything in this book to you with no expectation. If something doesn't feel right, or doesn't resonate with you, then move on. Trust your instinct and intuition.

That goes for the speed at which you read this book and the length of your healing journey too. Go at your own pace. If you feel like reading a few chapters a year is enough, then that's great! Who cares if it takes you ten days, ten weeks, or ten months to finish the book? I certainly don't. Try and release any judgement you may have about going on your healing journey in a right or wrong way. That doesn't exist. There is no set amount of time your healing journey will take.

While this book focuses on the sudden unexpected loss of a loved one, anyone who has experienced a traumatic loss, like a divorce or job, may find healing and guidance on their journeys too.

Whatever experience has drawn you to this book, please know that you are welcome here, and you have a place to belong.

"The Grief Prescription"

Grief is not logical, rational, or anticipated. It strikes us unpredictably. For me, especially in the beginning, it felt like some days I was standing waist deep in the ocean as waves calmly slapped against my stomach in a steady rhythm. But then there were days—sometimes minutes or hours—when suddenly the waves turned choppy, crashing and thrashing against me, and threatening to drag me under.

This is grief, and I can't tell you when this will happen to you, or how often, but it will. Know that it's okay, that it's normal.

Whenever grief rises up within, I want you to return to the *Grief Prescription* and implement *"The 3 B's."*

The 3 B's

Be in the moment. Forget about what you have to do, or what life will look like in a week, month, or year. Looking too far out into the future will only create more anxiety, depression, sadness, and anything else you can think of.

Breathe. Just focus on your breath going in and out of your body. Focusing on deep breathing will assist you in staying physically healthy.

Believe you are not alone. There are many people experiencing something similar to you right now, and many who have found a way through, just like me. You will find a way through as well.

If you only weave *"The 3 B's"* into your life, these practices alone can go a long way to moving you forward on your healing journey.

We Persevere

Healing is a journey, one that you deserve to go on.

While it may not feel it right now, you deserve to heal from the pain. You are worthy of moving through it and releasing it, of freeing yourself, and of learning how to pick up the pieces of your shattered life and soul.

You deserve to experience joy, and love, and gratitude

for life again. Your loved one would want that for you, I promise.

As I tell everyone I work with, your "A-Life" is gone. You and the life you knew have been forever changed by the sudden and unexpected loss of your loved one, and there's no going back. When this happens, life can feel heavy, it's dark, and the pain so overwhelming that you may wonder if you can go on living let alone ever feel joy, love, or peace again. I am here to tell you, yes—yes, you can free yourself from the darkness and pain and experience love and light, joy and peace, forgiveness and gratitude again (or perhaps for the first time).

Your life and Self have been shattered, but you can learn how to pick up those pieces and create a "B-Life" for yourself. It won't look or feel the same. It's not supposed to. Also, creating your B-Life isn't about creating a "better" life. It's about creating the "best" life you can after your loss; honoring every minute of every day. There is not one day, one moment that I wouldn't give my life for Logan to be here in physical form.

But those aren't choices I get to make, and it's not the world I get to live in. I share this with so much compassion for you, because I know how much we wish it. Our "B-Lives" won't be the same, because nothing will ever be the same again. The choices we do have are to stay trapped in the wishing for what was, or to move through our pain and grief and find what's on the other side. Who will we become? How will we live? How will we honor our loved ones and our Selves?

Having been on this journey for more than a decade, I can tell you that, through my connection with Logan, I have learned what it means to truly live, what it means to forgive myself and others, and what it has taken to free myself from the iron shackles of self-doubt, deep grief, and paralyzing pain. I don't think that I really knew what life was about before Logan's transition. I hold deep gratitude for the sacredness of life and the beauty of this world, and those are lessons that Logan continues to teach me every day.

It is my sincerest hope in the coming pages that you will find guidance, support, and the knowledge that you are never alone. Whatever pain or grief you're experiencing, the odds are that I have too, and so many of your unknown brothers and sisters are going through their own trials after the sudden and unexpected loss of their loved ones. Most of all, I hope you find solace and comfort as you undertake your healing journey and begin to create your "B-Life." The healing journey is intense, but it's worth it because the more you invest in yourself, the more you will experience the fullness of life again—the light, the love, the compassion, and the grace that is on the other side of the darkness and grief.

On this journey, may you find your light.

May you find peace.

May you find love.

And may you heal your shattered heart and soul.

Our journey begins now.

Part One

The Foundation

Chapter 1

Grief Will Steal Your Energy

"Ma'am, do you know why I pulled you over?" the officer said to me.

"No," I responded. I had been sobbing so hard that I'm sure my eyes looked red and puffy and my cheeks wet.

"I've been following you for ten minutes and you've been speeding. What's going on?"

"My son died, and I'm going home," I said matter-of-fact and without emotion. The officer's eyes widened. I could tell I had shocked him. The officer slowly nodded, then asked for my license and registration and walked back to the patrol car.

Apparently, I had been doing about 70 miles per hour in a 50 miles per hour zone. But I had no idea. I barely remembered getting behind the wheel. I knew I had made the 40-minute drive from my home to the office, but when I drove into the parking lot, I couldn't get out of the SUV. I sat behind the wheel weeping, and the tears wouldn't stop, so I texted my staff and told them I would be working from home. I remember leaving the parking lot, then nothing, just the blue flash of the patrol car lights in the rear-view mirror and the siren that jarred me from whatever stupor I was in.

I have no idea how long the officer was gone, but, when he returned to my window, he asked if I needed him to drive me home or if there was someone who could come and get me.

I shook my head. "No, I'm almost home," I told him. I was less than 10 minutes away I realized, when I finally gazed around and took in my surroundings.

"I promise to be more alert," I added as an afterthought.

He studied me for a moment then nodded. "Okay, well, I'm not going to give you a ticket, but it's unsafe to drive like this, so be more careful," he said sternly, like he was scolding me. Then his tone softened as he added, "And I'm sorry for your loss."

Life fades to black with the loss of a loved one.

There is a period immediately after our loved one has gone when there is so much buzzing and activity. We have funeral and memorial preparations to make. The phone constantly rings and dings as people call and text to check on you. There is the steady stream of food that often comes from neighbors, friends, and family. There are the many cards found in the mailbox from people telling you *"I'm thinking of you"* or, *"I'm so sorry for your loss."*

At some point though, the consolers return to their normal, everyday lives. For you, reality hits. There is no "normal" for you anymore. There is no returning to what was. This is often the moment when our grief really strikes, and it's just the beginning.

Grief is dark. It's deep. And there's no avoiding it. Some doctors say there are two kinds of grief. There is *acute grief* which happens in the first six to 12 months, and *persistent grief* which lasts longer than 12 months.[1] We often hear about the importance of seeking counseling and professional guidance, and I couldn't agree more. I started to see a grief specialist almost immediately after Logan's death, and I strongly advise people to seek out professional support, healers, and counselors.

But, what no one told me to expect was the heavy toll the grief would take on me physically, mentally, emotionally, and spiritually. During the first year after Logan's death, grief stole my energy in a way that still surprises me today. Most of the literature on grief says we may feel tired, but what I felt was a soul-weary, I-can-barely-do-the-dishes exhaustion that wiped me out. It was like I had lost all strength to even make it through my daily activities. Despite this level of fatigue, I couldn't sleep. Most nights, I tossed and turned. I felt the loss so strongly in my body, especially in my chest. The phrase "heart break" took on a new meaning for me.

What I've found in working with hundreds of people who have also lost a loved one suddenly and unexpectedly, is that this level of energy loss on multiple levels is common.

Intense grief can affect the body and mind in very real ways. Studies have shown that people who are going through intense grief only have so much capacity to handle day-to-day activities.[2] For example, if I was given 50 "resource units" of energy to use every day, 80-90 percent of my energy went into grieving, leaving me with only 10 percent to give to work, family, friends, social media, errands, and working out.

---

1   "How to overcome grief's health-damaging effects," *Harvard Men's Health Watch*, April 2018, https://www.health.harvard.edu/mind-and-mood/how-to-overcome-griefs-health-damaging-effects.

2 "Healthy Grieving," University of Washington, accessed June 2020, www.washington.edu/counseling/resources-for-students/healthy-grieving/.

When I was grieving, most of my energy went into just existing, just breathing. My physical capabilities were limited. My memory was limited. I did not have enough energy to do everything that I had once done. I felt drained all the time. I would do the dishes and want to go to bed. Five minutes walking outside left me needing to collapse—that's when I could convince my body to move at all.

When I was active, I didn't recognize myself. It felt like I had lost abilities and skills.

When Logan died, I was working for an organization that was incredibly supportive. My board of directors gave me three weeks of bereavement leave and paid my full salary for the duration. When I returned, they granted me the privilege to work from the office or at home, and a tremendous amount of flexibility—more than most people receive. I wanted to go back to work, because I needed to focus on something other than Logan, but it was difficult to concentrate and my capabilities were limited.

I remember being on a phone call months after Logan's death. I thought I was doing better and had significantly rebounded. During the conversation, I agreed to shoulder some responsibility, but when I hung up I had zero recollection of the conversation. I couldn't even remember who I had spoken with! Fortunately, I had caller ID which helped trigger a little memory, but I still had to call the person back and tell him how sorry I was, but that I couldn't remember what I had agreed to. (I still can't tell you what that was.)

When the day comes to return to the office or to begin some of your previous routines, be honest and forgiving about your abilities. You may have no memory. You may be unable to concentrate. You may forget words or trail off in the middle of a sentence. You may forget who you're talking to. You may feel like you can't reason, make decisions, or think like you used to.

You may feel utterly exhausted, like a deep, soul exhaustion most of the day like I did. Just getting out of bed in the morning may be a struggle. You may not feel like yourself. You may find yourself angry all the time over what would seem like silly things—a coworker who arrives late or pops his head into your office without knocking first.

Whatever you experience, know this: *There is nothing wrong with you.* If you're feeling such exhaustion that you can hardly move or think, then please know that these are normal and common reactions. It's your body and mind telling you that you don't have the energy or the capacity to show up and do what you used to. Gradually your energy should return, your stamina increase, and your mental fog should dissipate as the months go by and you begin to adjust to this new life.

For me and many of the people I work with, the first six months to a year are usually the hardest on the body, mind, and spirit. So, hang in there. Be gentle and easy on yourself.

If you're two or more years out from your loved one's transition and you still feel so low on energy and that you don't feel like yourself, that's okay too. You may want to seek assistance from someone on the outside, whether that's a therapist, energy healer, or another trusted professional who can help you work through the deep grief.

Personally, my energy has ebbed and flowed over the years even working with many different healers. That first year was terrible for me. There's no sugar coating it. During those 12 months, my brain also tricked me into believing that Logan was coming home, something that I know many of us experience in that first year.

But, as the second year began, my brain stopped tricking me as I started adjusting to this new world. I also invested more in my healing, and as I did, my energy returned on all levels. I physically felt stronger, and mentally felt more clear-headed. I could think more rationally, make decisions a little easier, and my memory slowly returned too. I also still experienced exhaustion.

Even today I have to watch my energy and be gentle with myself, especially during certain times of the year, like around Logan's birthday, the day he died, and the holidays. I've learned these dates can trigger grief—it's not as heavy as it was that first year, but it rises up.

It's easy for us to push this aside without recognizing what's happening. So, first thing's first, just acknowledge and accept that your energy may be limited, your memory may be shot, and your mind scrambled. When you feel drained, try to get enough rest, take a nap. Sometimes people forget to drink enough water and become dehydrated. I recommend limiting caffeine, alcohol, nicotine, and any mind-altering substances that could drain your energy more.

Remember to eat too. Food had no appeal to me, but if you can, try even small nibbles of fruits and vegetables, or easy-to-digest foods like warm soups and broths, maybe some plain rice. Try to eat healthy, whole foods and limit the processed, fast-foods. We want to nourish our bodies, especially in the early days of our grief.

Also, try going for slow, easy walks outside, or pick another very gentle and easy form of exercise. That could be yoga, Qigong, Tai Chi, or swimming. Gentle movement can help to move and release the grief that's in your body while also clearing the mental fog from your mind.

You may also find that these tips help generate more energy.

Just take it easy. Accept where you are. Be kind and understanding to yourself and give yourself permission to let your memory and energy slowly return at their own time.

• •

~ DAILY PRACTICE ~

Focus on your breath. That's all you need to do. Breathe in. Hold. Breathe out. Hold. In. Hold. Out. Hold. If it helps, you can count how long it takes for you to take a full breath, then hold it for the same amount of time, and then release it for the same amount of time. Try doing this practice five-to-ten times (or as many as you need). Repeat this practice as often as you need to throughout the day.

Fact: I still do breath work, especially when I feel grief or sadness come on.

• •

Chapter 2

Some People Will Disappoint and Surprise You

I couldn't understand why Paul wasn't grieving.

Paul wasn't Logan's father, but he and I had been in a long-distance relationship for more than five years. While he lived three-hours away, we would spend weekends together and talk almost every night. He had bonded with Logan and Ashley, Logan's older sister, almost as soon we started dating. Paul was a part of Logan's life, and I thought Paul loved and cared for my son too.

When I learned Logan had transitioned, Paul was my pillar. He was my strength. He made sure I drank water and put food into my body. He helped me make memorial and funeral arrangements. He flew with me to South Carolina, which is where Logan's father lived, and where Logan was living at the time he transitioned. As I look back, he cared for me when I couldn't care for myself.

Paul was steady and stable and solid, but I rarely saw him crack, and that made me so confused, sad, and angry.

I wanted to see him cry, to rage, to break down, to show some emotion, other than strength, like I had seen when his dad transitioned. I wanted to see that he was upset and that Logan's death affected him too.

But Paul showed me very little emotion. He said very little about missing Logan or being sad he was gone. He held his grief close to his chest and didn't show me his pain.

As the months passed I drifted away from Paul, and eventually I broke up with him. I was in so much pain I didn't have it in me to try making our relationship work, or to even talk about what I needed from him, or what wasn't working.

His hidden grief wasn't *the* reason we broke up—there were other reasons. As the years passed, I always felt such fondness and gratitude that Paul was in my life. I can't imagine how I would have gotten through the early months without him being a safe refuge. Still, for years I felt hurt by not seeing his emotions. At the time, I believed that if Logan meant something to Paul, then he would look upset, he would cry all the time and break down just like me. I was too wrapped up in my grief and my specific definition of how everyone, including Paul, *should* grieve. I really thought everyone grieves the same way and shows it similarly.

I was so wrong, and, as hard as it is to admit, it took me years to realize my mistake.

A few years after we parted ways, Paul and I were talking, and he mentioned how much pain he had been in. He'd wait until he was alone to break down. He told me that he hadn't wanted to show me his emotions, because he thought he needed to be strong in order to protect me.

"Why didn't you say something?" I asked, stunned.

"I didn't want to make it harder for you," he told me. He didn't want me to have to be strong for him. So, he kept all of his emotions in until he could escape to a bathroom or bedroom, or until he was in his car driving home.

The second your loved one transitions, your perspective on life changes, therefore your relationships change too. Some for the better and some not.

Some people in your life—people close to you—will probably disappoint you. You may expect someone to show up and be available for you, and when they don't, it hurts. Maybe it's your brother or sister, your mother or father, a dear friend, or your spouse or partner. Maybe you thought someone would send a card, or you expected them to call, text or reach out (even though you weren't picking up). Maybe you wanted this person to sit with you as you cried, holding your hand or hugging you close. Maybe you thought they'd listen as you talked about how much pain you were in and how much you missed your loved one. Or maybe you expected someone to give you more space. Maybe you wanted to be left alone, and they kept pushing and prodding you to talk about your feelings more than you wanted.

It's natural for us to place expectations on the people around us—most of us do it all the time without realizing it. We want our friends and family to show up for us in the way *we* want them to. *They should be able to see exactly what we need and then give it to us,* we may think. That was my experience with Paul. I needed him to show me emotion. I needed him to hold me while I cried and I needed him to cry with me. I needed to hear Paul tell me that he missed Logan and was in pain too. I expected him to show up the way *I* wanted him to, but I never communicated this to him. I never told him what I was thinking or feeling. I kept it all inside. I told myself a story about Paul that turned out to be untrue, and that was so unfair to him.

I'm not proud of how our relationship ended, and I

share it so you can learn from me.

I believe most of the people in our lives want to be there for us, but for whatever reason, they can't. Some friends may not fathom what you're going through, and so they have little to no sensitivity to your needs. Some people who were also close to your loved one may be experiencing tremendous pain and grief too. They're trying to find a way through their intense emotions, which may mean they don't have the capacity to be there for you too. For some people, it may be too difficult for them to see you in so much pain. Or, your loved one's death may trigger other unresolved traumas or losses that they never fully moved through, so this one adds more weight, more pressure, and more pain and they shut down.

Then there's the topic of death. The transition from the physical to the spiritual makes many people uncomfortable. In the Western world, our culture largely ignores and pushes aside conversations around death and dying. So, we're left ill-equipped to emotionally, mentally, even physically deal with the intense pain of grief and loss. Many people avoid it because it's too upsetting to think about.

There are so many reasons why someone may not be there for you in the way you want, expect, or need them to. This is not about you. It's not that they don't *want* to be there for you, it's that they don't know *how* and some people can't.

If a relationship is significant enough to you, then I recommend that you try talking to them about what you need. Tell them what you're feeling and would like to receive from them. This means you have to acknowledge that, and so you will probably have to tune into yourself and be honest. It's also okay to say, "I don't know what I need." In both scenarios you're opening communication, and that's really important as you work through and begin processing this sudden and unexpected loss.

Clear communication, especially around what you feel and need, gives people a chance to show up for you. It doesn't mean they will, but you've opened that door.

In hindsight, I wish I'd had the tools and knowledge to have told Paul, "It hurts me to see you not grieve, and I feel like you don't care." Had I said that, I would have at least given Paul a chance to tell me what he was actually going through, and the opportunity to be there for me in the way I needed, instead of me making up a story that just caused me, and him, so much more pain than we needed to experience.

No matter what happens, I find it helpful to keep reminding myself that the way someone else behaves isn't about me, it's about them. This is true for any reaction in life, really. When we understand this, it helps us stop any self-blame or extra pain we may layer on top of our grief.

The last thing you need is to mistakenly believe you've done something wrong. You haven't and neither has the other person. Both of you are doing the best you can trying to find your way through a very difficult and painful time.

Try to be easy and forgiving to yourself and others around you.

And this goes for the people who will make idiotic comments or asked questions that will make you see red. I can't tell you how many people asked me how Logan had died, like they wanted the details. Some people said to my face, "How did Logan kill himself?" Some people asked me, "Did you know he was suicidal?" A few people, in a condescending tone, told me, "He's in a better place."

These questions and comments were incredibly inappropriate and, to this day, I still can't believe people seriously say such things. But they will, and they'll ask other insensitive questions or make remarks that have you wanting to lay them out cold. You do not have to respond to anyone. You owe people nothing. You get to decide and control what you share. Feel free to say, "I prefer not to talk about this with you," and then walk away.

You may also encounter the people who will ignore what happened. Part of my job was to advocate at the State House, in Montpelier, Vermont, which meant I had to go into a building where hundreds of people moved through every day, many of them I had known for decades. Think of high school with different classrooms and groups, and a large cafeteria where everyone gathered, and you won't be far off from imagining what the State House is like. In fact, the inside joke was that it felt like being in high school, where everyone knew everyone, and gossip and information got passed around like a giant game of telephone.

I was so nervous to return to "the building" (that's short for the State House). I didn't know what I would say to people, or whether I'd suddenly get emotional. I also didn't want anyone's judgement or accusations. Some of my biggest fears were unfounded, since more people than not avoided me. These were people I'd known for years, and they wouldn't make eye contact when they passed me. Some people, when they saw me walking down a hallway, would make eye contact, but then they quickly ducked down a staircase or walked into a committee room.

I felt ashamed, and it hurt that people pretended like I wasn't there or that Logan hadn't suddenly died by suicide. It took me a long time to realize that they were uncomfortable around me and didn't know what to say. Again, it wasn't so much about me, rather their reaction to the situation. For them to say, "I'm sorry to hear about, Logan," was too difficult.

Just as people grieve differently, people will likely react to you and your experience differently too. And again, their reaction has nothing to do with you. It's not about *you*, it's about *them*. Many don't know what to say or how to act around us, and so it can feel easier to them to avoid or pretend nothing happened.

As hard as it is, try shrugging them off, or say a prayer for them. I know it's hard, but accepting people for who they are, and where they are, can be healing. If you get mad, that's okay too. Be mad! Write in your journal. Vent to a close friend or loved one who does show up about how challenging it is being around some people. Punch a pillow, go outside and scream. All of these are acceptable ways to release your emotions, and all emotions that get stirred are okay.

I'm not saying it's easy to understand other people, or fair. You shouldn't have to be the bigger person or do the work for someone. None of this is really about them; it's about freeing you up to focus on yourself. You do not need people in your life who are unsupportive, unable to show up for you, or who make insensitive comments.

You have enough pain and grief to deal with, so you'll want to limit any additional and unnecessary sources. As I said before, you have a limited amount of energy right now. Stay focused on using that energy for your healing. Be self-ish. Selfish is a good thing. It means you're taking care of yourself, putting your needs at the top. This allows you to stay focused on using your energy for your healing journey.

Allow People, Who Can, to Be There for You

You deserve to have people in your life who support you. You have needs, and you deserve to have them met. If you can't get those needs met by certain people, then you seek support elsewhere. That may require you to be open to allowing that support to find you.

Just as you'll be surprised by who won't show up for you, you will likely be surprised by who will. It could be someone you didn't know very well, or a casual friend who may come into your life in a surprising way and gift you with such kind and generous acts that you will never forget them.

That happened to me.

When Logan transitioned, I was living alone. Paul lived three hours away. My daughter, Ashley, was in college in South Carolina. While my parents lived close by, our relationship had been strained since before Logan's transition. Two of my closest friends lived out of state, one in Texas and the other in Massachusetts. Both came and spent the first few weeks with me, but they had to return to their families and lives.

I was back at work, splitting my time between the office and working from home, but I was spending a lot of time alone in my grief.

One day, while working from home—or trying to, unsuccessfully—the doorbell rang. When I opened the door, I was surprised to find an old State House colleague standing on my doorstep.

"I was thinking of you and wanted to see if you needed to get out of the house for a little and maybe go for a walk," she said.

I was floored. I would never have called this woman a friend. Friendly, yes. We had shared the occasional cup of coffee and conversation over our more than twenty years working in politics and government. But, this was not a woman I would have put on a list of, "people most likely to be there for me in a time of need." Also, it was a 45-minute drive from her house to mine, so she had clearly gone out of her way to find me.

I could have said no, and I'm sure she would have

respected that. But her showing up meant something, and I thought a walk outside would be nice. I don't remember what we talked about or how long she stayed. I do remember how her unexpected appearance made me realize that people cared, that someone was thinking of me, and that not everyone would be afraid to be around me.

There was another moment that also taught me this lesson. Many months after Logan's transition, and long after the condolence cards and letters had stopped, I found a card in the mailbox. It was from an attorney I had worked with at the State House. I had served on the House Judiciary Committee and worked on the landmark Civil Unions bill in Vermont in 2000. This attorney advocated for the bill. It had been almost a decade since we had interacted in any significant way.

Inside the card she had written such heartfelt words about how her heart ached for me when she learned about Logan. She also shared a passage from the book, *The Little Prince:*

"In one of those stars I shall be living. In one of them I shall be laughing. And so, it will be as if all the stars were laughing, when you look at the sky at night. I hope these words will one day give you comfort, just as they have given me after my father died."

To this day, reading her card brings tears to my eyes. I don't know what prompted her to send it months later. Maybe she had just heard the news. Maybe she had known what had happened but had forgotten to send it before and had just remembered. Whatever the reason, it didn't matter. She had taken three minutes out of her life to write a card, and that meant a lot to me.

Both stories remind us that unexpected gifts can come from unexpected people all the time. All we have to do is allow those gifts into our lives.

There will be people who can sit with you in whatever space you're in. There will be people who can support you, who will be there for you. Find them. Let them in. Seek them out. Lean on them. I promise you there will be people who can tolerate the pain and suffering without growing uncomfortable; who want to and can listen to your stories of your loved one. The key is to let go of your expectation about who these people will be and allow the ones who are meant to be there for you, to be there.

Know and trust that you deserve them.

. . . .

~ DAILY PRACTICE ~

Make a list of the people who have been there for you—anyone who has written a card, called you, shown up at your house, has sent you a gift, dropped off food, sat with you while you cried, helped you around the house, has gone for a walk or tea. This list can include people you had expected to be there for you, and those you didn't. It can include therapists, healers, mediums, and support groups too.

This practice will help you recognize all the people who are there for you (or were there), and the many ways they're showing up in your life now.

. . . .

Chapter 3

You Will Want to Make Changes ... Don't!

About six months after Logan's transition, I broke up with Paul, my long-term partner.

Two months later, I got into another relationship.

Four weeks after that (around the nine-month mark from the day Logan transitioned), I sold my home, and moved out of town into my new boyfriend's place.

This is my cautionary tale, my very own PSA (public service announcement). Please, don't be me.

If at all possible, stay where you are, and wait to make any big life changes during that first year after your loved one's transition.

There are reasons why many experts suggest we hold off on making major life changes, although we may want to after a significant loss. Our worlds have been upended. We have been uprooted. Nothing makes sense to us anymore. We will often feel unstable and unsteady. We're reeling from the sudden and unexpected loss, and we need to give ourselves time and space to grieve, to adjust to this new life, to work through the shock, and to come to terms with what life will be.

By delaying major life changes, we make one of the kindest, most compassionate, and, dare I say, sensible choices for our futures.

That first year, you likely will not recognize yourself. Three years down the road, you will probably be a very different person. Of course, that's often true for everyone. We all change, but I'm talking about a massive change, an altering of who we are on a deep level.

Just as your life will never be the same, *you* will never be the same. How you see the world, how you interact with it, how you feel about yourself, the world, and people around you, how you choose to spend your time, all of these aspects that make you who you are, will likely change.

I know every step that I've taken on my healing journey has been the right one, and my life has worked out the way it was supposed to. Still, I unintentionally caused pain to other people—and myself—because of my choices during that first year. I ended my relationship with Paul abruptly, and I immediately jumped into another relationship. Within six months, my new partner and I built a home together, and then we got married only to get divorced a few years later. I will always be grateful that my ex-husband was in my life, and for the support he gave to me in those difficult years immediately following Logan's transition. However, in hindsight, I realize I wasn't ready to be in another relationship so quickly. It wasn't fair to him or to me.

I didn't need a new relationship that first year, I needed stability. I needed a foundation under my feet and chance to feel grounded while I worked through my early, intense grief and learned how to accept my new reality. When we make huge, life-transforming decisions during this time, we can unintentionally create more instability and pain for ourselves and people we deeply care about.

To help you see clearly, I will highlight a few areas in our lives that, if you can, I recommend leaving untouched during that first year.

Your Home and Community

For the first six months following Logan's transition I dreaded stepping foot in the local grocery store. I lived in a small town where many people knew me and my children. I had also represented the town for eight years in the Vermont House of Representatives, had owned two businesses, and worked in a Vermont Governor's administration, so I knew a lot of people. I didn't want people's stares, their pity, and, what I was most afraid of—their judgement that I couldn't save my son. I was terrified that they'd see me and wonder where I went wrong.

I felt so angry, anxious, and uncomfortable shopping and being seen in my community that I ran errands, had dinner, and shopped in the next town over.

Sometimes we can carry a lot of self-blame, self-shame, and guilt over our loved one's transition. Sometimes we can agonize over what we could have done differently, what signs we may have missed, or if we had just said something else then maybe they'd still be alive. While I find this is especially true for those of us who's loved one died by alcohol, drugs, or suicide, those emotions or others can strike anyone.

For me, I had carried so much shame and blame about Logan's suicide that I believed other people in my community had blamed me too. This wasn't true. It was a story I made up, but, in my head, I had convinced myself that it was real.

Within that first year, I did move 45-minutes away to a new town with my new boyfriend. Again, in hindsight, I wish I had stayed and given myself a better chance to more lovingly release my home, Logan's room, and what that place represented for me. I was in such a rush to move out and leave the daily reminders.

If you can, I strongly advise staying in your current home and town. Also, try putting off relocating plans, especially those that would send you across the country or away from your existing support systems. I know the pull to seek a new start—you will, at some point. But right now, you will probably need and want your friends and family in that first year. Even if it doesn't feel like that or you don't think you need them.

I didn't want to see or talk to people. The only person I cared to communicate with was my daughter. But looking back, I realize how much I needed my support system—my close friends and the more casual acquaintances. Isolating ourselves is very common, and, while it's healthy to give yourself time and space to grieve and work through your emotions and thoughts on your own, too much time apart can be harmful. For instance, if you haven't left your home for more than 48 hours, then I'd suggest getting some fresh air. Go outside and be around people, even if all you do is people-watch.

If you can't bear to be around people——there are other ways to connect. You can call, text, or video chat. You can reach out to people on social media. I know being proactive to keep those connections may be hard, but they are worth it, I promise. It doesn't have to be long. Even ten to fifteen minutes can be all you need. Think of it as dipping a foot, or just a toe, gently into the water.

Every brief touch and encounter becomes a gentle return to human connection, to this lived, physical existence, which you remain an important part of.

After a year, if you need a fresh start, I get it. Have at it. Move to a different town or a new home. But in that first year, try and stay rooted in your house and community—they will ground you in ways you probably wouldn't expect or anticipate.

Your Job

When it comes to your job and employer, I advise you to stay put too. I remember wanting to quit. It wasn't because I had a different career or position in mind. I just didn't want to work at all. I wanted to be alone.

Thankfully I stayed. There was comfort in knowing how to do my job, whereas, when you switch jobs, there is always a learning curve. I can't imagine what it would have been like if I had changed jobs, had to meet and get to know new co-workers, colleagues, or a boss. My entire body shivers just imagining that.

I was also very fortunate in my position. My board of directors and staff were fantastic and treated me with the utmost respect and understanding. They were willing to work with me and were very understanding that there were days when I couldn't be in the office. I was given the flexibility to work from home, to change my work hours and schedule, and to take time off when I needed it.

Now, that's not always the case, but I encourage you to have as open and candid conversations as you can with your employer about expectations. Start those conversations as soon as possible and continue to check in with them throughout the year. Talk to them about what you may need and see if they are willing to adjust your work schedule, change hours, or job duties. Tell them about what you're going through, and how you're also committed to them, and see if you can find solutions that work for both of you. I've found most employers are reasonable and they want to help you, but they often don't know how.

If you've had these conversations and it's not working, or if you have a boss or you work for a company that is rigid and inflexible with you, then you may have to change organizations. I would still do whatever you can to try and make it through that first year while at your current employer, but your health and wellness needs to come first. If that means leaving, then do so.

And if you stay for the year and it's still not the right fit, or you're inspired to change jobs or careers, then consider taking steps in that direction.

Your Relationship

Earlier I wrote about my relationship, so this is the point in the story where I kindly suggest you stay in yours, if you have one. (Of course, if it is an abusive or unhealthy relationship, then please do what you need to stay safe by making any necessary plans that you have to.) This one may be hard, I know. People grieve to varying degrees, and I know the sudden and unexpected loss of a loved one can place tremendous strain on a relationship—especially when a child has died.

But, when you let go of a relationship, there's grief and mourning attached to that too. It's mourning what is no longer and may never be again. You don't need to torture yourself by piling on more grief right now, and that's likely what would happen if you left your relationship. If you need more time alone, then say so. If you need to spend more time with your spouse or partner, and you want to talk more, then tell them. The best advice I can offer is to be as open and transparent with your needs and in your communication as you can. And if you need help with that, there are professionals and counselors who can assist you and your spouse or partner.

Everything about your life will change and evolve because you will change and evolve. Losing a loved one suddenly changes you on a deep and profound level. But you won't see these changes or understand them for some time. I can't tell you what your life will look like three years, five years, or 10 years down the line, but I can tell you it will look differently.

Waiting to make huge life changes doesn't mean that you will *never* make them. Most of us will eventually. But in that first year, giving yourself the space to adjust to your new life takes a lot of energy and attention. Staying put so you can focus on your healing journey will help create a solid ground under your feet.

Focusing on breathing and communicating as clearly as you can with the loved ones in your life are some of the best actions you can take during this time. Those really are enough.

Whatever big life change that you may be drawn to, it won't fix or change what you're feeling. It won't lessen your grief or pain over your loved one's transition. That comes the more you invest in your healing and go on this journey.

. . . .

~ DAILY PRACTICE ~

Write down the date and then all the changes you
want to make in your physical world right now.
Next, put that list in safe place and don't look at it
for at least a month. After a month, pull out the list
and update it. Cross off what changes you may no
longer want to make or add new ones. Review it no
more than once a month. If you want to space out
the reviews even more, that's okay. As you do this
exercise, you will begin to see how your vision for
your future changes and, by the end of the year, you
will clearly see which changes are in your best interest and which ones were probably ones you wanted
to make in the moment to help ease your pain and
suffering.

. . . .

Part Two

Picking Up the Pieces

Chapter 4

Connect to the Divine

For my entire life, I've been drawn to the spiritual world. I've been baptized in or belonged to as many religions as I've had husbands (for the record, that would be three).

I've been searching for a connection to something greater than me. I've always believed there was something more to life, I just didn't know where it was or how to find it. No organized religion ever seemed to fit me; none *felt* right. I knew there was something more, something bigger than me, but I didn't know what to call it.

When Logan died, I wasn't affiliated with any religion or spiritual practice. My spiritual practice, if you can even call it that, consisted of reading spiritual and personal development books on how people overcame difficult situations and experiences. These books inspired me and gave me hope that I could get through anything because others did.

I often went to mediums for guidance too. I wanted an unbiased take on if I was making the right choices in life or was on the right path. For instance, I turned to a medium to validate my decision to get divorced, sell a home, and run for re-election in the Vermont House of Representatives.

But I didn't have an everyday practice that connected me to God, the Divine, Allah, the Universe (whatever term feels right to you). I didn't pray, meditate, or clear energy.

After Logan's death, I needed something. I felt this calling on a deep soul level, but I wasn't sure what that looked like. For me it wasn't organized religion. I didn't want to be judged, criticized, or left to feel that I had to defend my son in any way because he died by suicide. I didn't need to be told that how my son transitioned was a sin, and this is what I feared that I would hear.

I was also so, *so* furious with God. How could he have let this happen to me? How could he allow my smart, affectionate, compassionate, amazing son die so young? Turning to God wasn't comforting to me, and it didn't feel like religion would help me feel connected to Logan either.

Sensing I needed some connection, I started praying regularly, asking Logan to send me a sign he was okay, that he wasn't mad at me, and that he knew I loved him so much.

"Please give me a message, Logan," I'd say. "Please, tell me you're okay."

My prayers were answered. I saw signs, felt his presence, and got his messages.

Once I was standing in my kitchen talking with a friend when I heard a strange yowling. I turned and spotted Logan's cat, Hilton, who had jumped on top of the table. He was standing on his hind legs with one front paw against the wall for balance and the other tapping at a picture hanging on the wall.

The picture was of Logan.

I felt chills throughout my body. I had never seen Hilton do this.

Then there was the time I was laying on Logan's bed, playing cribbage, our game, when I heard Hilton start yowling from the doorway. In those first few months after Logan's transition, I always found Hilton in Logan's bedroom, but that night Hilton stayed in the hallway and he wouldn't step across the threshold. As I tried coaxing him in, Hilton suddenly vaulted across the threshold and started swatting at the air as he jumped around like he was trying to catch something. He kept yowling as he did this.

I knew Logan's spirit was in the room with us.

I started sobbing and rolled over onto my side. My heart felt like it was in a vice grip, getting tighter and tighter. Then I felt an arm drape over my waist as a long, lanky body curled up behind me. I sensed it was Logan and I was picking up his energy.

There was another time when my friend, Beth, drove to Vermont to pick me up and bring me to her home in Massachusetts. On our way there, we stopped at a gas station and a car pulled up next to us. I looked at the license plate and couldn't believe what I saw: *LV 33*. Logan's full name was Logan Voyer (LV) and his basketball number was always 33.

There was a morning when I was curled up in bed reading a book on how to survive suicide. I was crying. I wanted to talk to Logan so badly that I kept saying out loud, as if he was in the room, "I'm sorry, Logan. I love you so much," and that's when I suddenly heard this message from within tell me to "Call Brenda." Brenda was a Tarot Card reader who lived two hours away.

Without second-guessing it, I called her. She's usually booked months in advance, but she happened to have a cancellation for that afternoon, so I went to see her. I didn't tell her what had happened to Logan. I wanted whatever she was going to say to be real. As soon as I sat down, she said, "There is a young boy in the room with us who keeps saying, 'I'm so sorry!'"

"He keeps telling me that 'he loves you and is sorry that you are in so much pain. It's not your fault."

Hearing this gave me hope to hold on just a little longer. That if he was ok, and he wasn't blaming me then maybe, just maybe, I could find a way to not blame myself as well.

A month after Logan's transition, I had a strong intuitive feeling that I needed to call another medium, this one located in New York. I didn't tell this medium why I called her or anything about Logan. But, as soon as we were on the phone, she said she felt the spirit of a young boy in the room with her. "A young boy who keeps saying 'I'm sorry. I'm so sorry. I love you. I'm so sorry to hurt you like this. Had I known, then I wouldn't have done it." Again, this gave me hope that he loved me and he was saying that I couldn't have changed what had happened and that it wasn't my fault.

Receiving these messages through the mediums helped me to hold on in the moments when the pain was so excruciating that I wasn't sure I could survive.

They're Never Really Gone

From my experiences, I've come to trust that, although our loved ones may leave their physical form, they are always here with us. They're never far away. They're right by our side, and we can sense them if we're open to seeing, feeling, hearing, and believing them. For me, sensing Logan's presence and knowing he's with me has given me such comfort in those early years, and it still does today.

I also discovered that the more I invested in my healing, the more I noticed my connection to Logan and it felt stronger too.

The more we connect to the Divine (or if you prefer the Universe, God, or Spirit), the stronger our faith becomes, and we can use this to help us make important decisions. When I needed a sign, like if I was just feeling down about Logan, I'd say to him, "Will you please let me know you are here close to me?" Within minutes I'd get something, like his favorite song would come on the radio, or I'd look up in the sky and see a cloud shaped like his initials "LV" or a heart. I have lost count of the number of pennies that I have found in unlikely places too. I once asked for a sign from Logan, and ten minutes later I had opened the oven door and there was a penny in there. Did I mention my son was a prankster?

I talk with Logan regularly too. Every morning when I wake up, and every night before I fall asleep, I say, "I love you, Logan. Please continue to guide me along this journey." I know he does, and the more I know and believe this, the stronger our bond and connection grows.

Nurturing Your Connection

Connecting energetically with Logan was the first piece of my life that I picked up, and it supported me to rebuild my life and self. Developing a personal connection to the Divine also keeps me on my healing journey, it keeps me picking up the pieces even when I want to drop some of them.

Our lives do not always go as we plan, yet we can continue to make choices to move us forward. I know that every experience, even delays and pain are part of my path. I know it is not my human timing, it is Divine timing. There is a higher purpose for all of us. There is more to this physical existence than we often see, and when we cultivate and nurture our relationship to the Divine (by whatever name you call it) and the spirit of our loved one, then it becomes easier to accept our journeys through this world—whatever they may turn out to be.

For the first few years, I nurtured my connection with Logan through mediums. I needed someone to channel and translate his messages, because I had so much pain it blocked any chance that I had to connect with him directly.

Mediums can give you hope. I believe many of them have a true gift and can be a great source of knowledge and insight that we may not get anywhere else. Speaking with Logan through a medium allowed me to believe that there was a way to communicate with our loved ones even after their bodies are gone. It also affirmed that the signs I had been receiving were real.

If you don't use a medium, that is okay too. I know many people have turned to their religions and leaders who have helped guide them to connecting to a higher power. I'm purposely avoiding naming the Divine out of respect for all beliefs.

If you're interested in exploring working with a medium, then I encourage you to try it. I went to several throughout the world who knew nothing of me or Logan. Most gave me accurate information that they couldn't have known unless they were connected to something.

Whether it's a medium or religious leader, it's okay for you to try them and release them if they don't fit or work for you. I know many people who went on to explore different religions until they found one that felt right to them.

Eventually, I began exploring and nurturing a direct connection to the Divine and to Logan. It has taken focus and effort. I regularly meditate, journal, and spend time in nature—these practices have helped me cultivate my connection to the Divine. I've taken online courses, and I've attended events, conferences, and seminars hosted by some of the world's top spiritual teachers and mediums like Colette Baron-Reid, Dr. Joe Dispenza, Gregg Braden, Sonia Choquette, John Holland, Radleigh Valentine, Doreen Virtue, and Theresa Caputo. I've also studied under some of these teachers. I became a certified Tarot Card reader and have read hundreds of books on developing my intuition and connection to the Divine. I have studied several healing modalities and became Certified in Regenerating Images in Memory (RIM) and I'm now studying to be a Master.

I didn't know it at the time, but as I explored my connection to the Divine, it led me down a different life path where I now work as a transformational speaker and intuitive healer. Your exploration and finding a connection to the Divine doesn't mean that you'll wind up working as a healer (although you may!). More than anything, discovering your connection can help you find peace, acceptance, and forgiveness around the sudden unexpected loss of your loved one. It can teach you how to connect with them in spirit-form. No, that connection isn't the same as having them with you physically, but you can still sense their energy around you, you can feel their love and affection for you, and you can allow them and the Divine to guide you through life. For many of us, that's very healing and comforting.

Regardless of whether you're nurturing the connection to the Divine through a medium, your religion, or through your direct connection to the Divine or your loved one, you may find yourself walking a new, unexpected road that becomes a positive transformation for you.

. . . .

~ DAILY PRACTICE ~

To help you build your connection to the Divine, especially the spirit of your loved one, begin by asking and watching for signs. Sit in a quiet place. Close your eyes and take a deep breath in. Slowly exhale. Do this a couple of times and drop your awareness into your heart by following your breath in and out. Next, ask your loved one to send you a sign, one that you will recognize. I like to say, "Logan, I love you. Please send me a sign you're here and help me feel, hear, see or sense it." Then take another deep breath, slowly exhale, and say "Thank you, thank you, thank you."

If you want to sit quietly for a minute or two, then do so. Otherwise, you can open your eyes, stand up, and continue with your day.

Now, watch for signs. They arrive in different forms. You could see an ad for your loved one's favorite ice cream, or you may hear a song on the radio that reminds you of them. You may feel their presence like their energy is close to you. One woman said she saw her father sitting in the stands watching as she ran on the high school track early one morning. You could see certain numbers, or a particular book may fall from the shelf. Anything here is possible. All that matters is that you're open to seeing, feeling, sensing, and believing.

. . . .

Chapter 5

Find Meaning Again

It was late July, near my birthday, and just months after Logan transitioned. I had been at my office, but I was too upset to concentrate, so I told my staff I was leaving and drove to Logan's grave. It was more than a two-hour drive, but I went there often, especially in the early years. It was where I often felt the closest to him.

At his grave, I could scream and cry and write in my journal. I'd bring his favorite snacks, and I'd spend hours sitting and talking to him. Sometimes, I'd just lay on the ground and cry, begging him to hear me, begging him to know how much I loved and missed him.

That day I laid on his grave weeping and asking "Why? I am so sorry! I love you, Logan! Please forgive me, I'm so sorry!" I cried out. "What had I done in my life that was so bad that I was being punished? Why am I being made to go through this?" I asked the Divine.

I had overcome so many challenges in my life including early childhood sexual and physical abuse. As an adult, when my children were five and six, their father and I divorced. A few years later, he relocated from Vermont to South Carolina, so I effectively became a single mother. I never went to college, only earning my degree when I was in my forties by taking night classes at a local college. Yet, despite the challenges I had faced, I had succeeded.

There I was, and life felt so unfair and the pain was so immense that I didn't think I could handle it any longer. After Logan's death, it was my daughter, Ashley, who gave me the will to survive and keep living. I didn't want to go on, but the thought of leaving her alone, when she was already in tremendous agony, terrified me. I couldn't bear to think about taking my life and leaving her to suffer more pain.

Still, as I laid on Logan's grave, I didn't see how I could live with the torment. My actions had killed my son. I was to blame.

"Why? Why? Why me?" I cried out, sobbing. I was shattered and I had no idea how to put myself together, and so, at my lowest point, I begged the Divine to take me too. "Please," I cried, "I can't live like this anymore. Take me too. I don't *want* to live like this. How am I supposed to go on?"

I have no idea how long I laid like this, how long I pleaded and begged the Divine to strike me down. I hurt so much, it was like a car had fallen on my chest, and then a giant boulder on top of it. The guilt and shame suffocated me, and I didn't see a path forward. To me, I was trapped in a long dark hallway without any light, without any end.

Then, I felt this peace come over me. Even today I can't explain what happened or what it was, but suddenly I stopped crying. My body stilled. Then inspiration came. I received a message from the Divine. I heard it echo in my mind and felt it in my gut.

"If this happened in your life, then you're meant to do

something with it. Now, *do* something with it."

My eyes popped open. I heard that voice, and I knew it was a sign from Logan and the Divine. Suddenly, my mind started working again. For months I had lived in a daze, incapable of thinking or focusing for more than a couple minutes. I had zero memory. I could barely think clearly beyond the next breath, and thinking strategically about anything was off the table.

But my mind instantly cleared, I just knew I was meant to bring more awareness about suicide prevention to the public. I knew in my soul I had to help people, especially parents, recognize the signs of suicide—signs that I had missed. I needed to help them to learn the language to talk about suicide if they suspected their loved one was at risk.

After Logan had transitioned, I had spent hours scouring the Internet learning about the signs of suicide. I had to know what I did wrong, what I hadn't seen. We don't know, what we don't know. I thought, maybe if I had known the signs of potential suicide, I could have saved Logan; but since I couldn't change the past, maybe I could change someone else's future.

I had political, governmental, lobbying, and business contacts throughout Vermont who could help me make a real difference. I had media connections to journalists, reporters, anchors, and radio hosts. As a former state representative, I was also a public enough person that I knew outlets would pick up my story, if I was willing to share it.

I had the voice and the platform to do this work, and I was being called.

For the first time since Logan's death I could breath. I began downloading to-do lists and tasks. I could see who I needed to email and call, and I knew the very first outreach needed to be to the director of the Vermont Chapter on Suicide Prevention. I got in my vehicle feeling renewed and this shot of energy coursing through me. As soon as I got home, I called to set up a meeting with her.

I had a purpose: I was going to save lives.

Learning How to Live Again

For the next six months, I threw myself into the world of suicide prevention. It gave me a purpose to get out of bed each morning.

Most of all, it moved me, or rather, it moved my energy again.

When your loved one transitions, it can feel like life loses all meaning, color has turned to black and white, and all you feel is pain. You can feel slow; your body heavy and stuck. In the beginning, this is common. It's grief and pain and in a way, it's stuck in you. At some point, it's healthy to shift that energy and start to move it through our bodies, finding a purpose and meaning again.

As we do this, we start remembering what light and goodness in the world feels like.

We also find a reason to keep going because we are still here. There is a reason why you're here. You have a purpose—you just need to discover it.

For me, Ashley gave me a reason to go on living, but I also needed a higher purpose. I needed to find meaning and a purpose for this tragedy. That purpose became being of service in this world. I vowed to educate people about mental illness and suicide prevention because I desperately wanted to prevent other people from feeling the pain I felt. *If I could educate them about the signs of suicide, maybe I could stop people from losing their loved ones*, I thought.

You need to find a reason to live and a path back to life too (if you don't have one already). Living with the constant pain or numbness, isn't really living. That's being trapped in agony, in a terrible hellscape.

I know that you have a purpose for being here. You and your life have meaning. You matter. Your loved one's transition hurts, I know. And it can feel dark and desolate out there, like you're wandering through a night that will never end. I promise you, there is light in the dark, and there is light in every experience we encounter. Even when we're in pain, we can find something good to create from it—good for us, good for our loved ones, and good for the world.

Finding meaning and purpose again is your way back to life.

Everyone I have ever met who has lost a loved one suddenly and unexpectedly asks similar questions: Why? Why did this terrible thing happen? What am I supposed to do with this? What is the purpose? What is the meaning?

Finding your purpose and meaning in life can help you to answer these questions. At the very least, you will begin to find some comfort and hope.

Many Roads for You to Choose

Your meaning and purpose won't look exactly like mine.

Being of service has always inspired and driven me. I saw suicide prevention work as a natural extension to my time as a legislator. I loved those years as a public servant, so working on a cause and being of service felt right to me. But following my path by speaking publicly or giving interviews on radio and television may not be yours and that's fine.

Finding meaning for you will be unique to you. If your brother or sister died by suicide and your parents are still alive, maybe you go on living because you can't imagine your parents having to endure the pain of losing another child. Maybe you have other children or a spouse, or even a pet who needs you to get up and take care of them every day. It could be writing a book about your experience or getting involved with a cause or organization that holds special meaning to you or your loved one. It could also be finding something that you once loved to do but have let go, like playing the piano, drawing, cooking, gardening, bird watching, and reintroducing it into your life.

I drew from my background, so draw from yours. Discover *your* purpose and what's meaningful for *you*. Ask yourself: What can I create from this moment, no matter how big or small, that will make a positive difference in this world and in the lives of everyone around me? Then be open to whatever comes up, even if it's an idea or response you would never have imagined, like starting a nonprofit or becoming a mentor to at-risk teens.

Finding your purpose out of the tragedy and beginning to bring it into your life isn't a miracle drug. The pain you feel doesn't magically go away. The pain may still continue, but you can start to feel it lessen, or you may be reminded of what light and goodness in the world can feel like.

. . . .

~ DAILY EXERCISE ~

Rediscover what you used to love. Now is the time to remember what you loved to do. This is your pathway back to finding your purpose and meaning in life once more. If you want to get involved with a cause, that's great too. Go for it! Whatever gets you feeling a little energized, and gets you moving again in life, is what we're aiming for. If you bring this into your life every day, it doesn't have to take long. You can spend five to 10 minutes on it. What matters is that you add meaning and purpose into your life. This is the path back to feeling light and love again.

. . . .

Chapter 6

Invest in Your Healing

Once I realized my purpose, I dove in.

As soon as I got home from the cemetery, I emailed the director of the Vermont Chapter of the American Foundation for Suicide Prevention (AFSP) and asked her to meet. Over coffee, we created a plan to make their upcoming Out of the Darkness awareness and fundraiser walk, in three months, the best ever. I offered to use my connections with reporters to raise awareness about the event and suicide prevention by sharing my story.

Shortly after our meeting, I called a reporter at a top television station and asked if she was interested in doing a story on suicide prevention. She was. I was nervous to go on camera, but I felt it was my purpose and that I needed to give voice to people who often can't speak. As a society, we don't like to talk about death, much less suicide. I knew in my gut I needed to do this work, and so I swallowed my fears, my shame, and my insecurities and allowed the reporter and camera crew to come into my home.

This was one of the toughest interviews I had ever done.

I mostly held it together, but there were moments when the tears came as I talked about Logan's struggles with mental health, and I talked about the signs that so many people—myself included—often miss. I spoke about what we need to do to support our loved ones in difficult times, and for those who may have suicidal thoughts, to seek help.

As we wrapped the interview, the reporter said it was one of the most powerful experiences she'd had in her over ten-year career. There were times tears filled her eyes as we talked.

"This will change people's lives," she told me.

"I hope so," I responded.

The interview gutted me.

Every day, in every waking moment, I carried this heaviness in my chest like someone was always sitting on me, and tension in my shoulders. No amount of stretching, massaging, taking a hot shower, or using a heating pad ever eased it. When I went public with my story, the heaviness and the tension intensified beyond anything I had expected. It was like the grief I felt when I learned about Logan's transition had intensified.

Despite all the pain, I had to keep going and keep "doing" more. Some of my friends suggested we hold a fundraiser to raise money for our Out of the Darkness team, which we called "Team Logster." (Logster was my nickname for Logan.) I couldn't believe how thoughtful they were, and so we dove into organizing a benefit dinner and concert for the Vermont Chapter. We spent weeks arranging this. I was also busy raising money for "Team Logster" by soliciting donors and sponsors.

I was back to working full-time hours at my job and spending all my free time raising awareness for suicide prevention. I went from being almost immobile and struggling to function, to feeling like I had a purpose. There was a reason to continue living and that was to prevent others from experiencing the feeling of being in quicksand or drowning in a swamp because their child or loved one died by suicide.

I kept reaching out to reporters and media personalities, arranging interviews. I just had to reach as many people as I could to raise money and attention. I had to save people.

One of the interviews I did was an hour-long live radio interview on a prominent public affairs call-in program. That morning, my nerves spiked and the queasiness rose in my stomach that always struck me when I realized I would be seen. But I pushed it away. I didn't have time for those emotions. Instead, I did my hair and makeup, put on my jewelry and high heels, and walked into the radio studio, smiling.

I had known the host for years, so sharing our story—mine and Logan's—felt a little easier with him. I was getting more comfortable in telling our tale, but this format had live call-ins from listeners. People asked me what were the signs of suicide? How do you tell the difference between a typical teenage-mood swing versus depression? Won't talking to them about suicide put that thought in their heads? What were the signs of giving things away?

These were valid questions and I never faulted the callers for asking them, but each question forced me to reflect on Logan and what I may have missed and done wrong. Every question and answer felt like I was stabbing myself through the heart.

We ended the broadcast by sharing the suicide prevention hotline and asking people to call it if they are even thinking about taking their lives. "I know it's hard to feel this right now, but you are loved. Someone loves you and will be devastated if you're not here," I said.

It was hard to keep my voice from cracking or myself

from breaking down. I had tensed my body so much that my back ached. As soon as I walked out of the studio, I collapsed, sobbing in the hallway.

Sharing my story for everyone to hear and fielding their questions was so much harder than I had thought it would be. It was crippling.

In the weeks that followed I thought maybe I should stop doing these interviews, but then I'd get emails or messages on social media from parents who had heard me speak and how it helped them to talk with their kids. "Thank you for saving my son's life."

I heard from people who had thought about taking their own lives too. "I called the suicide prevention hotline when I heard your story and it saved me," people shared.

I was making a difference. I was helping people, and, more importantly, even in death, Logan brought meaning into this world. My efforts meant something, so I had to keep pushing myself to do more, to get back out there and raise more public awareness. So, I kept emailing my political and business contacts asking them to donate to the cause. My friends and I organized the benefit dinner and concert to raise awareness and money for suicide prevention. I was so proud of our work and yet, I started feeling resentful.

The world felt unfair.

I was making a difference in other people's lives, but *what about me?* I would think. *Why didn't I have the chance to hear someone talk about their experiences? Why couldn't I have had a chance to save Logan too? Why was my son taken from me?*

I couldn't stop the thoughts from coming, but I also couldn't let myself think about them too much, otherwise they would have dragged me down into depression's abyss. So, I shoved them to the side and kept working.

By the time the "Out of the Darkness Walk" happened, I had raised over $13,000. On the day of the event, I also gave a speech to hundreds of participants and volunteers, and I had arranged for the Lt. Governor of Vermont to speak at the event too.

It was the most successful fundraiser in the history of the chapter raising over $55,000.

We were so successful that the National Association for Suicide Prevention gave us the "Most Improved Chapter Award" at their annual event. I, along with a small group of volunteers, were flown to San Diego to receive the award and attend the conference.

I was proud of the work and effort I had put in and knew I played a large role in our success. It was grueling and difficult, but I was making a difference in people's lives! I was living my purpose!

But there was something about being at the conference that I hadn't anticipated. Every expert panel, every speaker highlighted the facts. For example, 90 percent of people who die by suicide experience a mental health issue.[3] That was Logan. For years, Logan battled mental health issues with different doctors diagnosing him differently and prescribing medications that left him with challenging side effects that altered his personality and moods.

I had seen all of these statistics before in my research after Logan's death. I learned about the signs and was educated, but there was something about seeing the stats and figures plastered on posters and in slide presentations projected on giant screens.

The numbers and stats hounded and hunted me. All I could hear in my head was a voice that said, "You knew

---

3 "Suicide claims more lives than war, murder, and natural disasters combined," American Foundation for Suicide Prevention, accessed April 13, 2020, https://www.theovernight.org/?fuseaction=cms. page&id=1034.

he had mental health issues. You should have done things differently. If you had, you would have saved your son's life. You could have stopped all of this. His death is *your* fault."

It got so bad that I had to hide in my room. It was the only escape I could find. All I felt was guilt, shame, and so much self-blame that it was too much to bear or to face other people.

How could I have not known?

When I got back to Vermont, I told the Vermont director that I had to step away from my active role in the organization. I also stepped back from fundraising and public speaking, including interviews.

Where once I had felt I had a purpose doing the suicide prevention work, now I felt *so* angry all the time. I had zero tolerance for anyone or anything. I began snapping at my friends when they complained about how they had to juggle work and make it to their daughter's basketball game, or they had to stay home with a sick child. *Be grateful you get to go to her game*, I'd think, or *At least you get to have a sick kid*. Everyone's problems seemed so minor and like nonsense to me.

I tried to keep my anger in check, but I couldn't. My impatience came out in my tone, in biting words, and in explosive rages. It wasn't reserved for a select few either, it was just about anyone who crossed paths with me at the office, at home, at the State House, or a store.

I'm used to debating people on their ideas. That's what I did as a lawmaker and I enjoy it. I like listening to other people's ideas and perspective and then challenging them with mine. But I wasn't challenging people, nor was I listening. I was reactive. "This is ridiculous and so miniscule," I once said during a legislative hearing. "It's nonsense and I can't believe that we're here wasting time debating this."

No one knew what to say. I had said it with such disdain and annoyance that I surprised even myself.

I didn't recognize who was talking. It didn't sound like me, but I couldn't stop myself either.

My anger soon turned into a deep sadness, almost a depression, but I didn't have time for that either. Instead, I started drinking more. Every night, I'd have a glass or two of wine. I told myself it was to help me relax, but really, I was just burying my feelings about Logan and myself. All my relationships began to feel strained. I stopped laughing. I gained weight. My body ached. It's almost strange to describe, but it felt like I was in quicksand. I couldn't move without being dragged deeper and there was no way out.

I was out of control.

One day, a friend made a silly comment to me—I can't remember what—and I lost it on her. It was a visceral, over-exaggerated response that flared into a fight that ended with me yelling and crying. To her credit, she didn't yell back. She waited, neither yelling, crying, or reacting at all. As I began coming down from my reaction she said, in a very quiet and calm voice, "Cath, I'm sorry, but I think you need help. You just seem *so* angry at the world."

I don't know whether it was her tone, her words, or something else, but I *heard* her. My behavior was so out of character and over-exaggerated. My reaction had been so explosive that it was impossible for me to ignore it.

My friend was right; I needed help.

Your Pain Is Still Inside

Finding my purpose was the thread that led me back into the physical world, yet underneath all my doing was an avalanche of pain that I hadn't addressed. It didn't matter how many interviews I did, how much money I raised in fundraisers, or how many lives I might have impacted. All my doing in the physical world didn't address my grief over Logan's transition, and I didn't realize it existed until it began manifesting in such explosive outbursts that I couldn't ignore it.

I had spent my life doing. When life got hard, I got myself out of it. I often threw myself into projects and work. That had worked for me in the past, so I subconsciously assumed the more I did, the better I would feel. That didn't work with Logan's transition—and, looking back, I'm not sure it ever had.

Everything I had done was with a pure intent and it did make a difference in people's lives. I'm very proud of the work I had accomplished. Still, the pain over Logan's transition remained trapped inside of me, because I hadn't directly addressed it. In fact, the more I dove into being of service, the more I used it as a way to avoid feeling the pain. I couldn't avoid my feelings forever. I carried them with me every minute of every day. They slowly simmered until my reactions to everything and everyone became so extreme, my anger so explosive, that I was forced to notice them.

I didn't like the person I saw reflected in the mirror. It wasn't who I wanted to be, and I wasn't living a life that honored my son. That idea bothered me, a lot. I was dishonoring Logan if I couldn't fulfill my purpose because I was so angry, ashamed, and guilt-stricken. If I couldn't be in public or be of service to others, then what was the point of Logan's transition? I was destroying the meaning of why my son had died, and that one thought focused me. I knew that I had to heal in order to live my purpose again.

I was in such agony and I couldn't find my way through that alone. I needed professional help, someone with whom I could work through my thoughts and feelings around Logan's transition. Still, I hesitated and felt unsure.

I had tried counselors and therapists before, and I had never connected with them. This time, I was so desperate to ease my suffering that I decided to try again, so I researched on the internet for therapists in my area who specialized in grief. I found Brooke, who used a healing technique called Cognitive Thought Therapy. That was something I had never tried and it intrigued me.

I didn't overthink this. I read Brooke's bio. I looked at how she described the therapy tools she used. I studied her picture, and then I called to set up an appointment. I had a good gut feeling about her, so I went with it. I consciously made a decision to face my pain on a weekly basis, one hour at a time.

It would turn out to be one of the best decisions I have ever made.

I worked with Brooke for years. She was such a gift in my life, and she absolutely helped me begin the hard, painful process of opening up and feeling my wounds over Logan's transition. She would go on to help me heal through other painful experiences that I'd had in my life too. I tear up thinking about Brooke and what a talented healer she is—that was how transformative working with her became for me.

It wasn't an overnight solution—I didn't suddenly release and move through all the pain connected with Logan's transition—but then, that's life, it takes time and the pace is often much slower than any of us would like.

We need a purpose and to find meaning through the tragedy, but that doesn't take away the pain we likely still feel. If we don't address what's inside, it festers and becomes an open wound, growing bigger and bigger until it gets so big that it prevents us from living our purpose, honoring our loved ones, and continuing our journey in this lifetime.

If you feel like you're living your purpose now, or that

you're keeping your loved one's name or spirit alive, then that's terrific. Keep doing that! Stay the course. You are *absolutely* helping more people than you can know, and you're doing the right thing.

And . . . you probably still need help.

Bringing your purpose into the world is amazing, it's awesome and wonderful, and I applaud you for taking that monumental step forward. Still, no amount of *doing* can heal you. Your purpose is not a magic pill. It will give you a reason to get up in the morning, to keep breathing, and it can be a life raft while you learn how to move through the pain.

But learning to move through the pain *is* something you must do. If you don't begin addressing it, then your body will likely break down. You may start experiencing physical ailments and poor health, trouble sleeping, impatience, anger, sore muscles, stomach and digestive issues, headaches, and in some cases, it could eventually lead to diseases, autoimmune conditions, and getting sick more frequently. Our bodies give us signals, subtle at first but then growing in severity, when we ignore our emotional pain.

Our relationships tend to suffer when this happens too. You may struggle more at work. Maybe you find yourself enraged by the smallest of acts or comments. Maybe you struggle with your children, parents, siblings, friends, or spouses and partners. It's like you cannot connect deeply and meaningfully with them and that takes its toll on you too.

The good news is that it doesn't have to be or stay this way. There is another way to live and it starts when you make a choice to consciously invest in your healing.

You Deserve to Heal

You deserve to heal!

This is such an important idea, that I'll say it again: *you deserve to heal.*

If you can, sit with that sentence for a few minutes. Put this book aside. Close your eyes and repeat the words, "I deserve to heal." If that feels like too much, then try saying, "I'm willing to heal." The word "willing" is like a bridge that can take you from your current place eventually into the fullness of deserving.

Were either of those sentences difficult to read or say to yourself? If you're in a place where you feel you don't deserve to heal, I *get* it. Gosh, do I. I was right there where you are. At first, I didn't believe I deserved to heal. In fact, I believed I deserved to be in pain. For a very long time, I lived with the belief that I had caused my son's death, therefore, I needed to pay a penance. Healing? No, I certainly didn't deserve that. And I certainly didn't believe it was even possible.

I was willing to accept this fate until it had affected my ability to honor Logan.

If you're struggling to move forward in seeking help because you believe you deserve to suffer, then ask yourself this: if your loved one was still here, would you feel they deserved to heal?

Of course, you would, right? You'd want that for them. You'd tell them to get whatever help they need, because they are worthy and deserving of it. You'd tell them they deserve to feel love again. The same is true for you. Grant yourself the same amount of compassion as I know you would give to your loved one.

Whatever you would give to your loved one, please, give it to yourself.

Your loved one wants you to heal through your pain. Your loved one is with you. They're walking next to you. Sometimes they're carrying you too, even if you don't know it. Your loved one wants to see you living. They want you to embrace your purpose and move through the world shining with the light of love.

This can only happen if you acknowledge the pain is real and then seek help in moving through it. In most cases, healing requires some deep work with trained counselors, therapists, a Shaman, energy healers, or support groups. You want to find people you can trust who will create a safe space for you to work through this pain.

There is no shame in reaching out either. Think of this as *investing in your healing*. This is about taking care of yourself—your mind, body, heart, and soul. It is about giving yourself what you need in order to go on in this world and honor your loved one. This work is life changing. Each time I have moved through the unknown that comes with a new healing modality, or every time I spent an hour consciously facing my pain by writing in a journal or meditating, I became lighter. It was like I moved through a layer of pain and I realized "Wow, this is freedom!" I wasn't healed, but some of the heaviness and the extra weight I was carrying slowly would disappear, little by little.

Over time, many years to be honest, it felt like I had moved from trying to walk through quicksand, then swimming through a swamp, then through a lake, to eventually feeling so light that I could walk on top of the ocean.

The Fear of Healing

There's one more area that I have to bring up that took me by surprise. It was something no one ever talked about. That was my fear of healing—of feeling and talking about my pain. A part of me believed that if I allowed myself to feel the pain, then I'd get stuck in it forever. Grief and pain, guilt and blame, shame and fear can feel like bottomless pits that, if you go into them, you'll drown. It's a very real terror, which is all the more reason to work with a professional healer.

You won't get stuck there, especially if you're working with someone who creates a safe and trusted space for you to explore your feelings. Over time, as you become more comfortable feeling your pain, you learn how to navigate through the difficult unexpected moments when grief takes you by surprise. The more you intentionally heal, the less afraid you feel as you learn how to dance with your emotions. I found that I stopped fearing my emotions and realized they were important indicators that gave me information.

Just give yourself time—however long it takes—and give yourself permission to work with people who were put here on this earth to heal.

. . . .

~ DAILY PRACTICE ~
#1: Write Out Your Pain

In this chapter there are two practices. The first one, is something you might be able to try at home and that's journaling. This is a practice I've used throughout my journey. It was one of the first I added into my life and one I still turn to today. For this practice, you will write what you're feeling and thinking. It doesn't have to be about your loved one. At first, it could just be what you're experiencing in the moment, and if that seems too difficult, that's okay. You can write about what happened during the day. There's no right or wrong way to do this. It's a practice that helps you reconnect to your inner self.

Journaling allows us to acknowledge our emotions and thoughts and to give them voice. We're so used to stuffing them down or shutting off our censors that sometimes it takes practice to recognize what we're feeling or thinking. If, at any moment, it feels too overwhelming, then stop. There's no forcing anything. If you don't feel ready for this, that's perfectly okay too.

The intention here is to give your emotions space, to allow yourself to consciously acknowledge what you're feeling, and to let those feelings flow through and out of you rather than bottling them up.

. . . .

Daily Practice #2: Seek Help

This is not a journey to undertake alone. There are so many amazing resources and trained professionals and experts who can help guide you, walk beside you, and support you through this.

Help can come in so many ways and forms. What works for me may, or may not, work for you. The key is to find what heals you best. Maybe that's working with a licensed therapist who specializes in grief. Maybe that's a virtual healing circle, or a bereavement support group. Maybe that's connecting with a spiritual healer or a religious leader. Maybe that's finding someone who does energy work or uses an alternative healing modality.

Seek out what calls to you, what fits your budget, and what feels doable. Remember, you can always try something, and if it doesn't work, you can let it go. Same thing goes for the person you're working with. You may find you like the therapy, but not the therapist. It's okay to try working with different people until you find the right person or persons.

The most important step is to try something and to keep trying different practices, modalities, and therapists until you find what works and feels like the right fit *for you.*

Chapter 7

Letting Yourself Laugh

I stopped mid-laugh.

I felt panicked and my heart pounded in my chest. *Should I be laughing? Is it too soon? What are people going to think: that I'm okay now? Because, I'm not okay. I'll never be okay.*

It was July 4th, and I was at friend's house celebrating. A bunch of us were sitting by the pool, sipping cocktails. It was a gorgeous summer day, and the younger kids were swimming in the inground pool.

One of the kids, who was about 5-years-old said something silly that made me laugh, but then I froze. I had so many conflicting emotions wash over me. I genuinely laughed, and it was one of the first times I felt so carefree and joyful since Logan had transitioned.

I felt terrified. I thought I shouldn't be laughing. What were my friends going to think? Did this mean I was forgetting Logan? That was impossible and I'd never allow that to happen. But, in that moment, I wasn't thinking about Logan. What did that mean? What did it say about me that, for a moment, my mind wasn't on him?

I second-guessed myself the rest of the party and for the rest of the night before I went to bed. In the weeks and months that followed, similar events played out. I never knew the "right" protocol. Should I laugh or not? Do I seem too sad? Are people annoyed with how down I seem? Are they judging me when I smile and I seem like I'm happy?

It was a constant stream of worrying and wondering, and I didn't know what was too soon, too late, too little, or too much.

Re-Engaging in Life

How do we engage in life again?

When is it okay for us to feel happy or to laugh again?

What is okay to show people?

These questions and more can torment us after our loved one's transition. There is no timeframe attached to when we can or should re-engage in life again. Re-engaging is the perfect description. There's a period after their transition when we're completely checked out. Then there are the periods spent trying to find a way to move in the world again, yet we can feel so disconnected. We don't want to engage. We don't want to watch a movie or television show, go out to dinner with a friend, help our son or daughter with their homework, or sit through another work meeting.

Nothing makes sense, and it all seems pointless.

But then we start to find our purpose, and then we seek help in moving through the pain. As we begin working through the complicated emotions around our loved one's transition, that pain starts to lessen a little, and as it does, it's like clouds parting just a tad to let a few rays of sun sneak through. We may discover moments when we're engaged in life again, and we didn't realize it.

We may watch a baby laugh, and we start laughing. We may be out to dinner or enjoying lunch with a friend and they tell a funny story, and we burst out with a deep belly laugh without thinking twice.

We are truly in these moments, living and enjoying them, but then, just as suddenly, as if we're being slapped across the face, we remember: our loved one is gone. It could happen moments after we laugh or much later in the day. We may feel our stomach drop as we're horrified thinking, *Oh, my God! What is wrong with me? Am I losing my connection with him? Oh, my God, am I moving on? Is this too soon? Am I supposed to be doing this?*

If I felt a moment of joy, I felt guilty and worried about what Logan would think. *Oh, my God does he think I'm moving on? Because there is no moving on. I'll never move on from him.*

I was also aware of the societal pressures. I was constantly afraid of being judged by others. If I laughed while in a meeting at the State House, I'd catch myself and would freeze just like at the Fourth of July pool party. *What are people going to think of me if I'm laughing? Am I laughing too early? Is it okay to laugh, ever? Am I supposed to show everyone how sad I am and that I miss my son, so I won't ever smile? Because I do really miss him and I need them to know I miss him.*

Feeling like we're moving forward can be one of the scariest emotions. There was a time when I worried that, if I let myself feel the pain and start to heal it, that I'd lose Logan again. Rationally, it didn't make any sense, but we're not rational after the sudden, unexpected death of our loved ones. I was terrified that I would have to "let him go" the more I healed. In a way, I believed the pain was all that kept us connected, so, if I healed, then it meant I'd forget him.

It's like survivor's guilt. We wonder if we're supposed to be living? Are we supposed to continue? Are we supposed to laugh or is it too soon? Are we supposed to smile or is that too soon?

The opposite can happen too where we wonder if we're mourning or grieving too much and we start worrying that we've waited too long to laugh or smile. *Will people think there's something wrong with me, like I'm stuck in this sad, grieving state?* I would sometimes think.

Figuring out how I was supposed to act was confusing and exhausting because there was no manual. No one sat me down to say, "Okay, Cathleen, here's your timeline, here's what you can expect, and good luck."

When I realized there was no manual, and none would be coming, I actually felt liberated. I could write my own and I could find what was best for me. At the same time, that thought terrified me. It meant I had to figure it out for myself. And I had to grow comfortable with the idea that what other people thought of me didn't matter.

Often, it's trial and error. We have to gauge every situation and allow ourselves to react how we need to. Those reactions can change from week to week, day to day and even minute to minute.

Yet, this is something we have to do to find a way to move through the world again, because life continues. Kids wake up and go to school, participate in their after-school sports, do their homework, and go to bed. Friends go to work, they change jobs, sell homes, and go on vacations. People get married, separated, and divorced.

The sun rises and it sets, and it happens day after day, and we are still a part of this world.

At first, realizing life goes on can be painful—you may not want it to. If you are like me, you probably want, more than anything, to go back to the way life was, to have your loved one back in their physical body. This is often true, even as you begin investing in your healing. But, as you move deeper into that journey, you will reach a fork in the road. It's the moment when you realize that down one path you can die with your loved one, not literally, but figuratively. Like a living death where you sleepwalk through the rest of your lifetime, never feeling connected to anyone or anything again. Never feeling joy, love, or peace.

Down the other path, is re-engaging in life.

Re-engaging means that you return to the land of the living; you return to feeling all of life again, the laughter and the pain, and by doing so, you honor your loved one too.

Laughter Heals

Laughter brings in the light again. It creates energy and moves it through our bodies. Crying does this too. It releases energy that has become pent up or stuck in our organs, muscles, and joints. It's why we say, "I need to have a good cry," and then we feel better after. Crying moves trapped energy and emotion that has gotten stuck somewhere in your body. Studies show crying also reduces stress and helps us to regulate our emotions.[4]

Laughter heals. According to the Mayo Clinic, in the short-term it soothes tension and activates our stress response.[5] In the long-term it boosts our immune system, relieves pain, and improves our moods.[6] There's science

---

4   Gračanin, et al., "Is crying a self-soothing behavior?" *Frontiers in Psychology*, 5, no 502, (May 23, 2014): doi: 10.3389/fpsyg.2014.00502.

5   "Stress relief from laughter? It's no joke," May Clinic, accessed June 4, 2020. https://www.mayoclinic.org/healthy-lifestyle/stress-management/in-depth/stress-relief/art-20044456

6 Ibid.

that shows that laugher opens the flow of energy in your system, stimulates your circulation, relaxes muscles, and creates endorphins, like laughter-yoga, where it creates a happier feeling. Just hearing a baby laugh makes you smile and you're like, "Oh, that's so sweet."

If you hear someone give a real belly laugh, it makes you want to smile and laugh; it feels good to hear that. It creates more joy within your internal system.

That joy also leads to something else: memories. For me and Logan, the last two years of his life were really hard for us. After his transition, for a very long time the only memories I could recall were the ones I had gotten "wrong." I remembered the moments when I had wished I could have said or done something differently.

Then I started laughing and feeling lighter (even for just a moment) and, surprisingly, a happy memory would pop into my mind. I found myself recalling these loving moments with my son, the shared laughter, the endless games of cribbage, the pranks he and his sister would pull on me, how he'd run to greet me at the door every night when I came home from work, how we used to make dinners together and eat at the table talking about our days. I remembered what a special bond we shared, and those memories began balancing my emotions. Over time, they helped me to see the bigger picture of my life and Logan's and how our two experiences came together in this world too.

Life is filled with both the light and the dark and everything that falls in between. That's true of every relationship in our lives, just as it's true of our emotions. Everything is combined in a cosmic, emotional swirl. You cannot just pick out one emotion and say, "This is all I will ever feel for the rest of my life."

For a while, I didn't believe I deserved to feel joy, just like I didn't deserve to heal. What I've learned is that allowing myself to feel joy again, allowing myself to laugh even if it was for a moment, opened new space for me to feel Logan again in a different way. Logan in his happiest, most centered, and grounded self was so playful. This was a kid who loved to joke around and make other people laugh. He was a jokester and a prankster, who lived to have a good time. That was who he was on a soul level, and so, the more I allowed myself to joke and laugh and play, the more I could feel my son's spirit shine through me too.

It was like he was there with me, laughing, joking, and playing again saying, "See, Mom, life is beautiful—enjoy it."

Pain clouds the warm memories and the deep, eternal bond and connection we share with our loved ones. Laughter parts those clouds and brings us back to life, to the world, and to our loved ones.

It's never too early or too late to let laughter into your life again or to re-engage with the world in a way that is authentic and right for you. I think one of the best ways we can honor our loved one is to be so present in a moment that we let it move us. We let whomever we're with, whatever we're talking about, watching, reading, or experiencing elicit an emotion and we feel it through our bodies. And, if you can, try and let go of the worries about what everyone around you thinks. What I've learned is that no one judges us as harshly as we judge ourselves.

You are still a part of this physical world—that is a great thing. You deserve to feel moments of joy and laughter, and it's okay to feel a little sad at the same time. You can feel both. It's okay, I promise.

~ DAILY PRACTICE ~

Laughing truly heals your soul.

It is a balm against the tremendous grief and pain you feel, and it's a way back to connecting with your loved one. So, find something that makes you roar with laughter, the kind of deep belly laugh that is genuine and authentic. Watch a comedy. Read a funny book. View a video. Spend time with little kids and watch them act silly and goofy. Just let laughter into your life, even if it's just a chuckle at first.

Laughter lights the way to joy.

Chapter 8

Creating New Traditions

I stood in front of rows of Christmas cards trying to find the perfect one for Ashley. The holiday music was playing over the loudspeaker and people milled about the small country store that was filled with books, tea cups, hats, scarves, mittens, wrapping paper, chocolate, and odds and ends. I really didn't want to be in this cozy holiday store. I didn't feel festive or like celebrating at all. I really wanted to find a card for Ashley, but I couldn't find the right one. I was getting frustrated, my eyes wandered, and I caught the label, "Son."

I froze. My chest got tight. My eyes welled up, and a sob choked my throat. I hurried out of the store so fast that I didn't give the young woman behind the counter a chance to finish saying, "Have a nice . . ."

I quickly walked to me SUV, threw open the door, slammed it behind me, and sobbed uncontrollably at my steering wheel.

A few days later, I returned to the store determined to buy a card for my daughter. This was a couple of years after

Logan's transition and, while I was doing well in coming to terms with my new life, I still missed him terribly, especially during the holidays. Even though I didn't want to acknowledge Christmas or celebrate anything, I couldn't forget about my other child. Although Ashley was an adult and living far from me, we talked every day. I knew she was still hurting too, and she deserved to have as much of a holiday as possible. Ashley still deserved to know that I loved her, cherished her, and was thinking of her during the holidays too.

So, I took a deep breath as I entered the store and swiftly walked to the cards. I told myself, *Cathleen, you can do this. You're doing this for Ashley.* I felt determined as I picked up each card searching. I glanced at the "Son" section, and, this time, there were no tears although the tightness in my chest was still there. Then something loosened in me as an idea crossed my mind.

Why couldn't I buy a card for Logan too?

I felt a mixture of sadness and a sense of connection with him, as I imagined finding the perfect card for him, sitting and writing to him just as I would if he were still in physical form.

Right there, I decided to find a card for him too.

Later that night, I made a cup of green tea and I put on soothing, instrumental music. I started the fire in the fireplace, and then I curled up on the couch and wrote cards to both my children.

I wrote how proud of them I was and how much I loved them. To Logan, I also wrote how much I missed his laugh, his bear hugs, and his egg McMuffin sandwiches (he loved cooking for his friends and family and he was really good at it). I wrote how I was sad that he wasn't physically here to celebrate this Christmas with us, but that I knew his spirit was watching over us and he was always guiding me. I wrote about my hopes and dreams for the coming year, and also what I was most grateful for in the past year.

I cried a lot while I wrote Logan's card, but, when I finished, I felt something release inside my chest. It was like I was letting go of a little pain just by acknowledging that it was the holidays and I missed my boy's physical presence.

I sealed Logan's envelope, and then I did something I hadn't done that first year: I hung his stocking next to Ashley's by the fireplace and placed his card in the stocking. When Christmas was over and it was time to take down the stockings, I left the sealed card in the stocking. I have added a card every year since and now have a special wooden box that holds all the letters and cards I've written to Logan.

Understanding Holidays

Navigating the holidays sucks.

At first, you may want nothing to do with any holiday. For me, that first year after Logan's transition, forget it. I didn't want to think, see, or hear about any holiday or event. I didn't celebrate anything—not Thanksgiving, Christmas, or New Year's. Ashley was in her twenties and lived in North Carolina, so I didn't have any children at home with me. If Ashley had been younger or lived closer, then I might have made different choices (which is my gentle reminder that your journey will look differently from mine, and that you need to honor what's best for you and your family).

I didn't address any major event until Logan's birthday. He was born in January, so not only did that first November through January feel like I was sinking deeper and deeper into the quicksand, it was also painfully obvious by the time his birthday came that I had to do something different.

I couldn't ignore the date, even if I had wanted to. Instead of seeing it as a celebration, I saw his birthday as a chance to thank him for the time he spent on earth in physical form, and to honor him in his spirit form too.

I love the ocean. I feel especially connected to Logan when I'm outdoors, so one night, as I journaled, the idea came to me that I could take a little of his ashes and scatter them in beautiful, magical spots across the world on his birthday. For his first birthday after his transition, I drove to the coast in New Hampshire.

Standing on the rocky shoreline, I held some of his ashes in my hand as I closed my eyes and said a short prayer. "Thank you, Logan for the gifts you have given to me and everyone who knew you. Thank you, for the time you spent with us. Thank you, for the time you spend with us now, and may you be at peace, knowing how much you are loved and cherished. I miss you. I love you, and you will forever and always be in my heart."

I cried as I said this, and then I let go of his ashes. As soon as I did, I felt his presence with me and I knew it was the right thing to do. Now every year, I plan a special trip to someplace magical and beautiful and I have a small prayer ceremony. Having a tradition around Christmas and Logan's birthday has helped to ease the pain that those days often bring, and it's given me a way to bring some joy back into those holiday moments.

Will the holidays be tough for you? Absolutely. They still are for me and it's been more than ten years since Logan's transition. Creating new traditions around important events has immensely helped me. It's been a way to keep Logan's spirit alive, to honor the life he had lived, and to know he continues to be a part of me and this experience. It has brought me more comfort than I realized it could when I first created this new tradition.

How I've celebrated the holidays and what they mean to me has evolved a lot over the years. How I reacted, responded, and experienced these moments has shifted as I've undergone my healing journey.

It's taken me some time, but I believe life is beautiful and that we are still here, in physical form, to experience its beauty, to heal, and to feel love. All that said, when the holidays and special moments come up, that doesn't mean we have to *celebrate* with balloons, confetti, and streamers—unless that's how you're feeling and want to celebrate, then go for it! To me, celebrating has become more about finding a way for me to feel connected to Logan, to honor him and everyone who holds a special place in my heart, to feel gratitude for the world we live in, and to be inspired to create more love, joy, and peace.

These special moments are also another way for us to honor and remind ourselves that our loved one's lives and their time on earth mattered, and they still exist in spirit.

New traditions also create space inside for us to experience the full range of emotions around the event and our loved one's transitions. It means we don't block, ignore, or pretend we don't feel anything—it means we feel it all. You're allowed to cry, laugh, and to feel whatever bubbles up inside of you. For me, my emotions are often mixed. I do feel joy, especially because I spend just about all the holidays and major events with Ashley now, and I am *so grateful* for our connection and the opportunity to make more loving memories together. And I still get sad that Logan isn't physically here to share those times with us. It's something Ashley and I talk about and acknowledge on those special occasions. Logan is a topic that is guaranteed to be discussed.

I can experience the joy of being with my daughter, the gratitude I feel for my friends and family, and the life I get to live, and I can still feel sad and I can miss Logan in his physical presence. I can still say, "I wish he could sit here with us, or be in the kitchen cooking dinner for us." I know he would have loved making a big holiday meal!

I try to allow whatever emotion I feel around the holidays to be felt, because that's how I continue my healing journey. You deserve to feel joy and to experience communion and connection with your friends and loved ones during special moments, while the pain can still exist. This isn't an either/or situation.

The pain will be there, and that's okay. Give yourself permission to feel that pain and allow yourself to create new traditions that fit you and your life today. Creating new traditions can help you move through whatever feeling you're having in the moment.

There are no right or wrong answers to what that tradition looks like. Trust your instincts and do what feels good to you and your family.

Maybe you set a place at the table for them during Thanksgiving, Christmas, or Easter (or whatever major holiday you celebrate). Maybe you serve one of their favorite dishes with a meal. And maybe it's different every year. It doesn't have to be the same exact thing each year.

Get creative. Find ways for your loved one to still exist in the physical world. For example, Ashley and I took a couple of Logan's favorite flannel shirts and created two stuffed teddy bears—one for each of us. This isn't connected to a specific holiday, but it's a way to honor Logan's presence which remains with us.

On his birthday, I go somewhere special that helps me feel close to him and honor my feelings. On his birthday, Ashley always bakes him a cake, because the last birthday we celebrated with him she made a horrible one—but he wouldn't tell her how bad it was, because he didn't want to hurt her feelings. Instead, he said he thought it tasted great. Now, she honors him with a cake that makes us laugh when we remember the story (and yes, there are still tears).

I get asked often about how to acknowledge the day our loved one transitions. I always respond the same: however you feel is best. I block off the day Logan transitioned, because I don't know what that day will bring. Often, I go for a hike or I'll plan a few days away at the ocean. Every year looks and feels differently. Some years, I have felt really sad and I have missed him terribly. Other years, the sadness is there, but there's a deep reverence for life and this experience that I'm having. It's hard to know in advance how we'll respond, so be kind to yourself and focus on creating what you need to honor your loved one, while taking care of yourself too.

I say this a lot, but please be easy on yourself, especially if you don't feel like acknowledging any occasions. It's okay if you need a break or it feels like too much of an emotional strain for you. Especially, for those first few years, you may want to skip the holidays. The only caution I offer is, if you find yourself skipping and ignoring holidays for many years, then you may, at the very least, want to try tiptoeing into celebrating a little, and if it's just too painful, then that could be a sign it's time to seek more professional help. We will grieve and feel a sense of loss, and sometimes that can turn into a depression, so we want to be aware of the line between, so we can take care of ourselves.

Our loved ones don't want us to mourn forever. They don't want us to be filled with so much pain that we cannot see or experience love, or joy, or connection ever again. They don't want us walking around like zombies—detached from our families and friends. They want us to heal. They want us to feel gratitude, peace, love, and happiness, which is something the holidays are meant to bring to each of us.

~ Daily Practice ~

Pick one holiday, special event, or milestone and write a letter to your loved one. Tell them about special moments during the year, your hopes, wishes, and dreams for the coming year, and thank them for being with you. In your letter, you can thank them for any signs they've brought to you, and how they've touched your life. This is a way to acknowledge their existence, and to honor them and you for the journey you've undertaken over the last 365 days. Then, create a special box or place to keep the letters you write to them.

Chapter 9

Give Yourself Permission

"I have some exciting news, and you're the first person I'm telling!" said Chrissy, one of my oldest and dearest friends since high school. Chrissy lowered her voice and leaned forward on the table as if she had a big secret to tell me.

It was about five years after Logan's transition and we were enjoying our weekly dinner. We had done this before Logan's transition. The first year after, I hadn't felt up for these meals, but during the second year, I had, and I always looked forward to them.

Chrissy burst into a grin. Her eyes sparkled and she blurted, "Samantha's pregnant! I'm going to be a grandmother!"

"Oh, my God, Chrissy! This is incredible! I am *so* happy for you!" I said, grinning back.

I knew how much Chrissy was looking forward to having grandchildren, and my heart felt so full of joy for my friend and Samantha, who I knew would be a fantastic mom.

For the next nine months, it felt like I got to live

Chrissy's joy too. She updated me on all the details from doctors' appointments, to how Samantha's pregnancy was going (lots of morning sickness in the second trimester), to finding out she was having a baby boy. I got to celebrate with my friend that a new life was being brought into this world and I loved it.

Having a child is a gift, and the joy of bringing life into this world is truly a miracle. I had always loved my children, but it wasn't until Logan transitioned that I understood how precious life truly is. The wonder of forming this tiny being inside of you, carrying them and feeling them connected to you for nine months, then giving birth to them, and watching as they grow and develop . . . there is nothing greater. It's beautiful and amazing, and I got to both witness and be a part of it again through Chrissy's eyes and joy.

I even helped her organize, plan, and decorate for Samantha's baby shower. We had so much fun! I loved being included and sharing that moment with my friend, and I couldn't wait to see the look on Samantha's face when she walked into her baby shower.

The night before, I went to bed feeling blessed and grateful for Chrissy and this life that I was living.

When I woke up the next morning . . . I could barely breathe.

My body shook, and I felt sick to my stomach. My head pounded, and I was sweating. It felt like I was about to hyperventilate or have a panic attack.

What was happening to me? I wondered. At this point in my journey I had more tools. I grabbed my journal and I wrote about every emotion that I was feeling. Then I close my eyes and focused on my breath. After a couple of minutes, my severe reaction subsided a little. I knew I had to look within myself to understand what was going on, so

I allowed myself to be curious and started looking at why, and where, this response came from.

Within a couple minutes, it was pretty clear: I didn't want to go to the shower.

All I could think about was how I would never have this experience with my son. *My son is never going to become a father and have a child. My son will never get married. He's not going to go to college. I will never celebrate a new job, a marriage ceremony, or the birth of my grandchild with him,* were the thoughts that raced through my mind.

I was very aware that there were no more "nexts" for us, and the baby shower slammed this home for me. It wasn't the first time any of these thoughts had popped up, but it had been years since I thought of them, and the strength and intensity of my feelings surprised me. It was like someone had taken a sledgehammer to my heart again. I felt the intense loss over Logan as if it had been yesterday, and that bothered me just as much as all the reminders of what I didn't get to experience with him on earth anymore.

Holding the Light and Dark

Through the therapy and energy healing work I had done for years, I was at a point where I could feel true joy for Chrissy. And, simultaneously, I felt the intense pain that I would never get a chance to experience something similar with my son too.

I didn't have to choose one emotion or the other. I could be happy for Chrissy *and* feel sad for myself.

As you begin moving through the pain, you will *feel* again. You will feel joy. You will laugh. And the pain will still be there. Sometimes it'll feel stronger, or it will last longer. You don't know when or what will bring it on, but there will be moments when it will hit and you have to navigate through it again.

You have permission to feel joy *and* pain. It's okay. It's also okay to feel whatever you feel in any moment, and for that to change too.

That morning, I did not want to go to the baby shower, but I also did not want to stay home. I took the middle path. I called Chrissy that morning and said, "Chris, I'm so sorry, but I'm feeling really emotional today. I am so excited for you, but I also know that I'm feeling pain. I don't want to create a scene, so if I leave early, without saying anything, just know that it's not about you; it's about my need to take care of myself and create some boundaries around my heart."

"Aw, Cath, it's totally okay," Chrissy said with such kindness and compassion. "Thank you for letting me know. I'll see you later."

That was our conversation. Just being open and honest with Chrissy about my feelings and what I may have to do released anxiety and reminded me that, while I may not be able to control what emotion gets turned on, I can control how I respond.

I was able to get dressed and go to the baby shower feeling a little more centered and in control of my tears. In the end, I did leave early, but not because I was going to have a breakdown. I just knew that I'd had enough and that, if I stayed much longer, I would likely have melted down. I knew my limit, and I accepted that, respected it, and took care of myself.

As you go through this journey, you will have peaks and valleys. You will experience the light and the dark. You will find joy and sadness.

Please, give yourself permission to hold it all—the light and the dark, joy and sadness, the peaks and the valleys. Then give yourself permission to act accordingly, even if that means changing your mind and making a different decision at the last moment.

If you've committed to going to a graduation party and, on the day, your emotions feel raw, it's okay for you to stay home. Or if you get to the graduation party, and you feel yourself starting to break down, it's okay to leave.

Your emotions can, and probably will, quickly shift, and there's no predicting what you'll feel or when. A song may come on while you're out to dinner and its instant tears and you have to leave. It happens a lot to me. I'll be in the car driving with the windows down, my sunroof open, it's over 80 degrees, and I'm feeling so grateful and happy, and then Logan's favorite song comes on the radio and I'm a wreck. I'll pull over or turn around and drive home because I need to let myself cry. Once the tears have stopped, I'll re-evaluate what I need and, if I have to, I'll change plans. Whatever your emotions are in the moment, It's okay. If you feel sad, it's okay. If you feel joy, it's okay. If you fight with your husband and then five minutes later, you're laughing with your son, it's okay.

Your feelings are not open for judgement. They are what they are, and they will change moment to moment. Go with it, because when you do, you allow the energy to move. Emotions are really just energy that moves like waves through our bodies. It's only when we try to dam up the emotion that it gets stuck, creating more pain that will eventually need addressing. By allowing the full expression of what we're feeling to go through us now, we allow ourselves to keep healing and moving forward on this journey.

No matter what, be kind to yourself. Be compassionate. Be forgiving. Be accepting of the full spectrum of your emotions. When you do, you honor your loved one and your Self.

~ DAILY PRACTICE ~

Sometimes it's hard to identify our emotions and to just be with them. I find that walking in nature helps. For this practice, you'll want to find a quiet, natural setting where you feel safe, secure, and peaceful. As you walk, notice what's around you. Take five to ten minutes and just focus on one leaf, a twig, a rock, a cloud, a branch, a tree. This moves you into the present and focuses your attention there.

Once you're grounded in the moment, then try identifying your emotions. "I feel angry," or, "I feel sad," or, "I feel anxious," or, "I feel happy," or, "I feel excited." Close your eyes and go within your body and "feel" what you are feeling. Identify where the feeling is within your body. It may be in your shoulder, your neck, your chest, your belly. Just notice where the feeling is being held. Then, take a deep breath, imagine breathing into that area of your body. As you exhale your breath, imagine the emotion being released with it.

There is no judgement on what you're feeling. If it helps, think of them as waves. They're temporary. They come in, and they'll go out.

Chapter 10

Build A Healthy Morning Practice

For most of my life, I had drifted toward energy healing and inner work. There was always a pull and a fascination for it. It was like something inside of me strongly resonated with messages, insights, and intuitive wisdom.

When I think about my more than ten-year odyssey since Logan transitioned, I believe it's been successful because I mixed conventional therapies, like Cognitive Thought Therapy, with studying and seeking treatment from alternative healing modalities. I've worked with Shamanic practitioners, an intuitive business coach, and energy healers. I've participated in Ayahuasca ceremonies in Costa Rica (Ayahuasca is a hallucinogenic that indigenous people of Central and South America have used for spiritual healing for thousands of years.)

I'm even studying to be a Master RIM facilitator, which is one of the most beneficial healing modalities I've used. RIM stands for "Regenerating Images in Memory." As the RIM Institute explains, it's "a body-centered, transformational technique that frees you of negative thoughts, feelings and memories, so you are empowered to live your best life. The RIM process allows you to re-generate your neurologically grounded sense of self in a profound way."[7]

In many of the healing modalities I've studied, I've learned about the benefits of maintaining a healthy mind, body, and spirit. I think we all know this is important, but it's *how* we do it and *what* it looks like that can trip many of us up.

It takes focus and commitment to create a healthy routine, but the benefits are so worth it. Shortly after I began work with Brooke doing the Cognitive Thought Therapy, I created a morning ritual for myself that I've consistently maintained for years—although the specifics of what I do have shifted. Every morning, begins with three keys:

- Some kind of movement or exercise.
- Some quiet reflective practice.
- Nourishing my body with a healthy breakfast.

This routine is my way of starting the day in a centered, balanced, and peaceful state.

Every morning I wake up and the first thing I do is write a gratitude list of ten things I am truly grateful for in my life. When I get out of bed, I do something physical. For the first few years, this was a quiet, contemplative walk outside in the woods or down a dirt road. I didn't listen to anything. It was just me and Mother Nature. I felt the air, noticing if it was cool or warm. I felt the dirt and grass crunch under my shoes. I watched the birds who flitted from the branches. I noted the gnarly bark on trees.

I was practicing mindfulness and training my mind to be in the moment, present and watchful instead of allowing my thoughts to sweep me into the pain of the past or the

---

7   The RIM Institute," Dr. Deb Sandella, accessed May 17, 2020, https://www.riminstitute.com/the-rim-institute/.

fears and anxieties for my future.

When I came inside, I would meditate. This was so hard at first, and, like a lot of people, I had to start slowly. I sat for less than five minutes for weeks—I couldn't focus or sit without fidgeting. I did it every day and over time I built up to sitting for 20 minutes. Sometimes, I'd put soothing, relaxing music on in the background to help calm my mind. Other times, I listened to guided meditations that taught me how to focus on my breath, exhaling and inhaling, and clearing my mind. How long I meditated in the morning depended on how much time I had, but I made sure I always sat for at least five minutes.

My morning routine also consisted (and still does) of listening, watching, and reading positive, uplifting material. Before I began this journey, I used to get ready for work with the morning news on in the background. I'd read the newspaper headlines or I'd scroll through my phone or social media accounts wanting to know what was happening in the world.

But most of the news that gets reported is dark, sad, and fear-driven. Instead of feeding the negativity and darkness into me, I began watching Wayne Dyer videos on the computer. Before heading to the kitchen to make breakfast, I would also stand in front of the mirror, look myself in the eyes, and repeat affirmations like, "I am love. I am lovable, and I am loving," that I learned from Louise Hay.

For breakfast, instead of grabbing a pastry or something sweet, I started making healthier choices like scrambling eggs with lots of vegetables, eating wholegrain bread, and drinking tea instead of coffee.

I didn't know it at the time, but my new, healthy routine was teaching me how to be still with myself, and it became the foundation on which my healing journey has continued. As the years have gone by, I've changed some of the practices, like I do full-body workouts or I go for a run in the morning instead of walks in the woods, but the core parts remain.

Start Your Day Uplifted

Every morning, I wake up and think of Logan. There isn't a day that's gone by when that hasn't happened. I'll admit, sometimes I still feel sad—really sad. I'll feel angry that he's no longer here and bitter that I won't get more moments with him. Those intense feelings, while I honor them, could also easily pull me into a dark place and that isn't how I want to go through my day. I want to create every day and every interaction with everyone I meet from a foundation of peace, love, and appreciation rather than anger, sadness, and bitterness. Having a healthy morning routine has helped me constantly move through the heavy feelings of loss and reach a place of inner peace, so I can move into the world, interact with people, and take action from that place.

What does your morning look like? If you're like many people, maybe you scroll through your phone from bed, checking out the latest scary news headlines, or maybe you flick on the television, computer, or radio to catch the morning news. In small doses, this is usually fine for people, they can handle, process, and integrate the negativity. But after a sudden loss, you're highly reactive, raw, uncentered and unbalanced. Feeding more negativity and fear into your mind, heart, and body is just destructive, and it sets you up for a very difficult day.

Your irritability and anger will likely be heightened, so you could easily and quickly find that you snap or lose your patience or temper with people. Your decision-making process could be compromised too. Just think about the times you've made choices out of anger, impatience, or sadness, were the outcomes what you had hoped? Did you get what you really needed? I know I didn't. I often would regret having made a decision or snapping at someone out of anger. I lost my patience with so many people and later I'd feel disappointed in myself for lashing out.

We can put ourselves on a different path, when we start our days with a routine that uplifts us. When we do this, it can bring greater peace, calm, and connection into our lives. A healthy morning practice centers, grounds, and connects us to our Divine selves too.

When we leave for work in this space, then our days may go easier. We may have fewer arguments. We'll feel less annoyed as we're not triggered as often. We may find that we hold onto our tempers better, becoming more patient, and able to speak more calmly.

When we become more peaceful and loving, that energy ripples into the world. And you, the beautiful shining soul that you are, will shift how you engage with the world around you. String enough mornings like this together, and you steadily move yourself into a higher, lighter, more peaceful consciousness.

It sounds amazing, right, so how do we start?

It begins as soon as we wake. We have to shift our morning habits. Habits become programmed and you can change them at any time. To see what I mean, try this: open both hands and then fold them together. Notice which thumb is on top. It's probably your dominant hand. Now, switch the position of your thumbs. Does it feel uncomfortable with the other thumb on top?

It probably does, but that doesn't mean it's wrong. You're just not used to it, but if you did this practice three times a day for 10-14 days, I imagine it would start to feel comfortable.

It's the same idea with your morning practice.

"But, Cathleen, I don't have enough time for a morning practice," I hear those words from the people I work with often. Resistance is normal, and you really do have the time, you just need to make it. You need to prioritize you. Lay out how you're spending your time.

Are you checking social media in the morning? Cut that out. Are you watching tv? Cut that out. When we feed that much negativity into our awareness, it changes us. It can make our energy weaker. Even negative thoughts can pull us down. Next time you grumble about the upcoming stressful day, stupid employees, or how much you're dreading the daylight, pay attention to how you feel. Notice if your body feels heavy, or if a body part hurts.

When our energy is weak, or we're feeding lots of negativity into our systems, it can make us more susceptible to emotional swings and being triggered by intense feelings of grief, anger, and sadness. Let me be clear: it's okay to feel those emotions. Feeling your emotions is healthy. What's unhealthy is when we're holding them in, or we become so reactive to them that they control our behaviors and how we respond to the world and everyone around us.

Also, notice what time you get up. Can you get up 10 minutes earlier? At first, that's all you need. If you can't wake up earlier, can you go to bed earlier, so you can give yourself that extra ten in the morning? Are you making breakfast for the kids, or your spouse or partner? If so, can your spouse or partner pitch in, or can you get the kids' breakfast ready and laid out the night before? Are the kids old enough to get their own?

These are the kinds of questions and solutions you need to look for, because your health matters. It's vitally important that you feel grounded and centered, especially after your loved one's transition. I know that feeling secure again can be hard, and it can feel like you take one step forward and three back, or you're taking just teeny steps forward.

There is no race. You have time to adjust your morning routine one small shift by one small shift.

And please know that just as you deserve to heal, you deserve to feel lighter, happier, and more peaceful too.

There is so much in life to be grateful for even after your loved one's transition. In some ways my ability to appreciate the beauty of this world, the fragility, the power, and the grace has exponentially increased because of Logan and his transition. I know, that may be tough to imagine right now, it's probably hard to feel an iota of gratitude. I get it. For so long, I felt angry at the world and a higher power that would "steal" my son from me.

So, if you're in a place today where you doubt or can't imagine this world as holding beauty, grace, and love, that's okay. I certainly didn't at first. It wasn't until I started to invest in my healing by working with my therapist and exploring different healing modalities that I did. And that was a few years after Logan's transition!

What I have learned and I believe with all my heart is that love, appreciation, and beauty will return as you move through the pain and begin releasing it from your body. Pain is like a solar eclipse—it blocks the sun—but when it starts to move, the light returns.

When the light begins returning to your awareness, like you notice it and feel it even if it's for just a minute or two, then you start awakening to how amazing your life still is, and can be.

If you've recently suffered your loss, then it's probably going to take some time before you regain that feeling of joy and light. That's common. It took me about three years after Logan's transition before I started to really feel those slivers of light, almost like the clouds parted just enough for me to feel the rays. Please, be gentle and kind to yourself. Give yourself all the time you need to grieve and move through the pain.

And know that this journey isn't all or nothing. You can feel sad and a little joy at the same time. You can wake up in the morning missing your loved one so much, and then you can go outside for a walk, or sit in meditation, and feel a moment of peace. There is no right or wrong to how you feel.

No matter how dark and sad you feel right now, there will come a point, and you will know it, when you're ready to shift ever so slightly to allow not just the light to come into your life, but for you to become lighter and to share that with the world too.

A large part of the healing journey is about finding emotional equilibrium and restoring your vibrancy, power, and light after experiencing such a sudden and profound loss. As your energy strengthens, you feel better, lighter, stronger, and ready to live your purpose, honor your loved one, and remain true to yourself.

Creating a healthy, uplifting morning practice is one of the best ways to slowly open your heart again. It allows us to set the tone for the day we want to have, to possibly connect with our loved one's spirit, and to help us along our healing journey.

· ·

~ DAILY PRACTICE~

The two most important practices to begin building a new healthy morning routine are: a gratitude list and affirmations.

Every morning, as soon as you wake up, write 10 things you're grateful for. Anything goes. You can write, "I'm grateful for the air I breath," or, "I'm grateful to live in this home," or, "I'm grateful for my husband/wife," or, "I'm grateful for this warm blanket."

Even if you don't quite feel it right away, just writing down the first thing that comes to mind. Noticing them will start to shift your energy. Eventually, you will feel the warmth of deep appreciation spread through your chest.

Next, mix in 10 positive affirmations that you say to yourself in the mirror like Louise Hay taught. Some of my favorite sayings are, "I am strong," "I am healthy," "I am kind," "I am powerful," "I am healed," "I am clear-sighted," "I am compassionate." Be creative.

There are many other ways to build a healthy morning practice. You could go for a 15-20-minute walk outside (one of my all-time favorites). You could write in a journal. You could meditate or do yoga. You could read a peaceful, spiritual book. You could listen to gentle soothing music while you make a cup of tea and just watch the sun come up. Depending on where you are in your life, like if you have kids still at home, this may take more creative work, but it's still so worth it for you.

It can include switching from coffee to tea or adding more vegetables and whole grains to breakfast while getting rid of starches and carbs. It could also be that you eliminate or reduce consuming scary news headlines.

Keep this simple. Pick one to two items to begin building a new practice, then add to it as you feel ready for more. Whatever you do, please don't pick eight new activities—within three days, you'll stop. You're creating new habits, so start small, add as needed, and carry on.

Above all, have fun! Changing your morning routines can have a profound effect on your entire day, wellbeing, and life—so let it.

. . . .

Chapter 11

Listen to Your Inner Guidance

My morning routine changed a lot over time as I experimented with different practices. Eventually, I added some to my evening routine too. But, no matter what time of day, three activities have stayed with me since the beginning: meditating, journaling, and walking in nature.

These practices play multiple roles in my life. First, they help me to release whatever difficult emotions or thoughts that I'm having. Second, they help me make sense of the events and experiences of my life, and bring me greater inner peace, understanding, and serenity. Finally, they help me to connect to my higher Self, the Divine spark that's within all of us. Some people call this our soul, others our higher wisdom or higher self.

I call this my inner guidance system.

The more I engaged with these practices, the more I found myself receiving messages about my purpose in this world and how I could be of service again. After my initial work on suicide prevention, I took a three-year hiatus to focus on my healing. During my morning practices, I began noticing this urge I felt to speak out on emotional pain. Specifically, I found myself being called to talk to other people who had suddenly and unexpectedly lost a loved one, the inner pain and torment, and how everyone deserves to heal and feel love. I kept feeling that I needed to help people learn to deal with their emotions in a healthier way, and that part of my journey was to share my story.

I'd be deep in a meditation and I'd see an image of me working with others who had lost loved ones suddenly and unexpectedly. I saw myself helping them to heal through their difficult and challenging emotions. Some mornings, I'd be on a walk, listening to the birds, breathing the fresh, clean air and I'd get this sensation that I was meant to be doing more than just running an organization. I had such vivid images of me standing in front of a crowd and talking about Logan's transition and my healing journey. I saw myself helping people emotionally heal by doing intuitive readings for them.

It felt like it was time for me to start thinking again about my role as a speaker and healer, so I could help people learn to pick up the pieces of their shattered lives, and put them back together again.

I'd feel so uplifted, inspired, and like a warm ray of sunshine was falling across my chest. I'd get tingles up and down my arms and legs, or shivers throughout my body. It just felt *so right* to me.

Awakening to Your Inner Guidance

Our inner guidance has a lot to tell us. It offers us strength in times of doubt, insight into how we can handle difficult situations, and what decisions and directions in life are in the highest and greatest good for ourselves—and by extension, everyone around us.

Our inner guidance also reveals to us what no longer works in our lives. We've all tolerated people and situations long past when we probably should have let them go. We've put others ahead of ourselves, and let our needs and desires take a backseat. As you work to heal through your pain, you realize that *you* matter—your needs and wants and desires are important.

This isn't being selfish. It's about recognizing that you haven't been listening to your inner guidance and have probably been fighting against it. The moment you step onto your healing path is the moment you start taking care of yourself—possibly for the first time. As you do this, often relationships, situations, and experiences shift. We gain greater clarity on what's right for us and what isn't. That clarity comes because we're tuned into and listening to our inner guidance.

You could be meditating, walking in nature, painting, or writing and you may get a thought, or see a vision, or hear a phrase or a sentence. It could be that you sense you need to change your diet, maybe you need to take out sugar and sweets, or to cut back on meat, or eliminate dairy.

Maybe you get a sensation that there are people in your life who are toxic to you, who drag you down every time you're around them. Maybe your inner guidance tells you it's time to let those friendships and relationships go, and to allow yourself to bring new, healthier ones into your life.

Maybe your inner guidance tells you it's time to make a career change by going back to school, getting trained in a new area, earning a different certification, or switching jobs or organizations. Maybe you hear your inner guidance tell you to try a new healing modality, or you have a vision of yourself doing yoga or taking up a new hobby. Maybe you hear it's time to move to a new home in the same town or to relocate.

There's no end to what your inner guidance has to tell you.

When you listen to your inner guidance, you're tuning into and listening to your heart and soul. It comes from your core, and your core is love—that is your connection to the Divine. Your inner guidance is light. It soothes, heals, inspires, and uplifts. It makes you feel the endless possibilities for your life and the world around you.

When you connect and can listen to this inner voice, you often feel more loving toward yourself and others. This connection helps you feel inspired to explore and experience all that life and this world has to show you. You want to be engaged in it—despite the pain and heartache you've suffered after your loved one's transition.

Our inner guidance is not to be confused with our inner critic, which comes from a more negative space. It's that little voice inside us that tells us we're no good, that judges us and other people, and that tries to keep us in the comfortable known. The inner critic can trigger shame, anger, blame, and fear. When your inner critic is advising you, you will feel heavy and dark, maybe even sad, angry, and hopeless.

On the other hand, our inner guidance helps us to *feel* our way through choices and ideas, rather than thinking our way through them. Often, our inner guidance will give us messages that may not be rational, logical, or make a lot of sense in the traditional way. For instance, when I meditated, my inner guidance kept telling me that it was time to be of service again. I would have visions of me speaking in front of groups and audiences, and by helping people emotionally heal by doing intuitive readings.

My first reaction was, *Hell, no! That's not logical, that's not possible, that's not in my plan, that's not what society says is right. What would my friends, colleagues, and family members think?*

I had no idea how I'd even do that. I ran an association. I was a former elected official and had worked for the Governor. I had built my career in a very different sector. At first, I shrugged off these messages as foolish daydreams and impossibilities.

But the messages kept coming and the images were so vivid, and they just *felt* right to me. I got tingles and shivers throughout my body when I allowed myself to imagine what my life could look like. Then I started to wonder, *What if? What if I did this? What if I spoke out? What if I helped people emotionally heal? What if I gave intuitive readings? I had always been drawn to the spiritual world and the New Age movement, so what if I became a part of it?*

I started to see these changes as possibilities. I wasn't sold on them yet, but I began visualizing myself in those roles. I allowed my inner guidance to speak to me through my feelings. This became easier the more I invested in my healing because I started clearing out more of the pain. The more pain you release, the more you can feel that light and hear your inner guidance.

After living through your loved one's transition, I know, this can be hard. There's so much pain trapped inside that we don't want to feel; we prefer to shut down or to build so many walls around our hearts that we can't feel anything.

Often, we erect these barriers unconsciously; they're a defense mechanism, and it makes a lot of sense. We unconsciously believe we're protecting ourselves. Except when we close off from the pain, we also close off from our inner guidance. That's why healing through our pain is so important. The more work we do to release our pain, the more we can feel the light. The more we feel the light, the closer we can get to reaching our inner guidance—our hearts—and being able to hear the messages it sends to us.

These are important messages that guide us to create a new life for ourselves that honors our loved one and aligns with the person we've now become. Our daily practices offer us a path back to reconnecting, maybe for the first time, to our wise, inner self. What you choose—whether it's writing, meditating, being in nature or something else—doesn't matter. Choose. Just pick something that you connect with and will practice consistently every day.

The more you do, the easier it is for you to access your inner guidance. Eventually, you may not need the practices to help you connect. You'll have access to it all the time.

When you do connect and receive a message from your inner guidance, there's no time limit for when you need to act. In the beginning, just practice sitting with and listening to what's coming through. Get comfortable with connecting inward, and learn to differentiate between your inner critic and your inner guidance. Then you can work on feeling comfortable hearing and receiving the messages your inner guidance sends to you. When something comes through, you can say, "Thank you, for sending this to me. Thank you! Thank you! Thank you!" Then relax and feel it, sense it, be in it. Try imagining what it would be like to act. Notice how you feel. Does it resonate with you to take that action? If so, then it is possible that you are meant to move forward with it. You will continue to be guided along the way.

Be patient. I spent months getting the same message about speaking out and helping people emotionally heal during my meditations. I didn't act on anything right away, I allowed myself to grow comfortable with the idea. The more comfortable I became, the more excited I became too. That excitement created the energy that I would eventually use to bring that vision into the world.

As you learn to listen to your inner guidance, continue investing in your healing therapies and your healthy daily practices. Eventually, you will reach a point when you realize it's time to take that next step in whatever direction you've been guided. You'll know it in your gut or heart.

Think of this period as slowly lifting a lampshade off your heart. Hour by hour, day by day, breath by breath you are returning to your center, to your inner Self, and ultimately to the Divine. What a beautiful journey that is.

~ DAILY PRACTICE ~

To really hear our inner guidance, we need to be in a quiet, calm, reflective place, free from distraction, loud noises, and interruptions. Start by looking at your new morning practice and focusing on your breath as you close your eyes and become aware of it flowing in and out. Consider added meditation, quiet walks outside, or journaling to your daily practice. These are three of the best ways to create a clear channel between you and your inner guidance. If you haven't added any of these, try picking one and set aside at least 15 minutes every morning to practice.

Remember to be patient too. It takes consistent practice to drop into the space where you can hear, feel, or sense your inner wisdom. Consciously choose you, one practice at a time.

Chapter 12

Step Out of Your Comfort Zone

What was I thinking? Why did I believe I could do this?

I stood in front of about a dozen people gathered in a small conference room in the basement of our local library. They were all staring at me as I began telling them my story about Logan. For an hour I shared with them the pain and struggle that came from Logan's suicide, and what it took for me to consciously step into my healing journey one hour at a time.

At first, my voice shook, but, within a few minutes, I settled in. I told them about my zig-zagging path through healing. I told them about my struggles to continue and to find new meaning and purpose after my son's transition. Most of all, I talked to them about how much they mattered, and how much they deserved to heal from their pain and grief too, and they were worthy of feeling love.

I finished by sharing tips about how to make this journey a little easier on themselves, mindsets to adopt, like not taking on blame or responsibility that wasn't theirs to shoulder, and why it matters that they continue to live their lives to the fullest.

The hour flew by and, before I realized it, I was taking questions from the audience. I felt so proud to stand up and speak my truth and also, perhaps, to give the audience hope and inspiration to go on their own healing journeys.

As the questions slowed down, one woman raised her hand. She had cried through most of my talk. I watched her try to collect herself as the woman next to her rubbed her back. Between sobs, the woman told us that her teenage daughter had died by suicide the week before and she didn't know how to go on or what to do.

The rawness in her voice was so clear and it was all I could do not to burst into tears too. I ached for her because, when you've lost a loved one to suicide, especially your child, it's a very specific pain that only those who have walked that road truly understand (and that's the case for so many experiences in life).

"First, I don't know if you're getting professional help right now, but if you're not, I encourage you to," I shared with her, putting as much compassion in my voice as I could, so she could hear me deeply. "There are many resources, some of them free, that you can turn to depending on your situation. I strongly encourage working with a grief specialist, if you can. There are bereavement groups too, that many people use. Next, just breathe. Consciously focus on your breath and getting from one to the next. In time, if you do this and get help, the pain will lessen. You deserve to heal and you deserve help."

She sobbed and dabbed her eyes with a tissue as I watched everyone else do the same.

That night, I collapsed on my bed when I got home. I felt drained. It had been more emotional than I had anticipated speaking in front of people and yet, it had felt so right. What were the odds that a woman would come who had so recently lost her daughter?

For months I had felt pulled to do this work, to step out from my comfort zone and to start speaking in front of small groups. That night, I did and by doing so, I set in motion a chain of events that would, years later, lead me to leaving my executive job, running my business full-time, working as an intuitive healer, certified RIM facilitator, and a certified emotional success coach.

Take Action

As you learn to listen to your inner guidance, what will you *do* with the messages you receive? At some point, maybe that's today, maybe it's tomorrow, maybe it's in a few months, but eventually you will find yourself ready to act.

It doesn't have to be a huge act. It can be a small step in the direction of the message. This is a turning point moment. It's the moment when you realize you can no longer continue living the way you had before, that it's time to change, that it's time to let your life and Self open up in new and different ways.

It's a shift from the intense sadness and grief into the next steps you can take towards where you can feel light, joy, and love once more.

Up until this point, you've picked up various pieces of your life and Self. Here is when you start putting them together again to recreate a different version of your life and Self. Usually, that means taking an action that you've never taken before. It's outside of your comfort zone. It's stepping through the fearful thoughts of, "I can't do this."

I'm here to honestly tell you, if I could do it, "Yes, you can."

You can because you know that your life will never be the same. Now it's about honoring your loved one and your

Self. When you consciously step through the fear, the life you live is beyond imagination. You will start to trust yourself and the messages you receive more, and as you do, life becomes easier. It flows easier. You feel happier and, most importantly, you feel the connection with the Divine, and possibly your loved one too. I have. I feel the connection to Logan very deeply.

As I stepped into and through my fear, it helped me to feel even more gratitude for the life I was living. For the pearl within the oyster that came from such intense trauma. Suddenly, there was meaning in my life again. I started to walk differently, talk differently, and I stood differently. I showed up in my life differently.

The more I worked through the layers of pain, I freed myself of heaviness, pain, and judgement. Now, I am not suggesting that this happens quickly. In my experience, we have layers of pain that need releasing, as we remove them, we can start to see our light. And the more our light shines, the more we can assist others on their paths too, because we have more to offer and share.

When we act on the messages from our inner guidance and we move through our fears, we start walking a path to love. We create our new life now from this place instead of from a place of anger, pain, fear, shame, and blame over our loved one's sudden and unexpected loss.

For months, I had received consistent messages from my inner guidance. I knew I needed to return to the public space, but I wasn't sure where to start. Becoming a transformational speaker, helping people to heal, and giving intuitive readings was a huge jump from running a major trade association, working in government, and being a politician. I wasn't sure what my friends, family, and colleagues would think of these new ventures either. Peer pressure, the need to fit into our tribes is very real. Any time we start to step outside and change, it can create some friction and tension in your existing relationships, especially if they don't change.

I wanted to live my purpose—I knew I needed to—but there was still fear. Instead of letting that fear hold me back, I decided to take baby steps in this new direction. I took an online class learning how to read and interpret Tarot Cards. I did this quietly and privately. I didn't tell anyone about it because I didn't want to hear any doubt or negativity. I also didn't know if the people in my life would support me. I felt drawn to energy work and healing, so I delved into it more with a friend of mine who was an energy healer, and who helped me begin to understand how important it is to feel the energy flowing into and through me.

I knew I needed to at least try, so I signed up and fell in love with the class. It boosted my confidence as I practiced reading other students. I also felt empowered and inspired, partly because I was doing something different in my life.

As I took the class, I also decided to organize my first public speech. I had done live radio and television interviews, but this was different and it took a lot of small steps to get me in front of the crowd at the library. I had to write a speech. I had to find a venue. I had to advertise. And then, I had to show up! For a quick second I thought about canceling—I was that terrified—but I knew in my heart that was the direction I was being guided to walk. I didn't know at the time where it would ultimately lead me, but I knew it was a path I needed to follow.

The first public speech, although it was hard, gave me the confidence to keep going. The woman whose daughter had died by suicide, later sent me a note saying that I had changed her life, which, in turn, changed mine. It made me realize that I had to stay open, to keep talking about my struggles and sharing my story. If I could help other people like that woman, I needed to.

From that point on, I kept taking small steps in the direction that my inner guidance encouraged me to go. I held more public workshops and gave more speeches. I did more intuitive Tarot Card readings. Over the next six years, I slowly built my work from a side hustle into a full-time private practice and small business as a transformational speaker, a certified intuitive success coach, an energy healer, a certified RIM facilitator, and a #1 international bestselling author. (For those wondering, this was about eight years after Logan's transition.)

None of this would have been possible if I hadn't faced my fears, one hour at a time, continued to move through my healing journey, and kept taking one small step outside my comfort zone after another. Even today, I have to keep taking uncomfortable steps, but the more I do, the more I feel like I'm being of service, fulfilling my purpose in the world, and honoring my son and his legacy.

Every step I've taken has also boosted my confidence and trust in the messages I receive. When you're just starting to tap into and connect to your inner guidance—to the Divine—it's very easy to discount the messages you receive as impossible, outrageous, or unreal. But when you start listening and taking steps and you see the results, you start to think *maybe there is something to this.*

And while many of the steps I took were scary, and I felt terrified and nervous after I took them, I felt brave and confident. I felt proud that I was stepping outside of my comfort zone and into this unknown world. Each step I took opened another opportunity to go another layer deeper into my healing process.

No one says you have to follow your inner guidance. But when we ignore it, then we can make our lives more difficult. Instead of embracing the new life we're being encouraged to create, we fall back into the old place—which is often a stuck, limbo-like existence. We're trapped wanting to go back to the old life, which is gone.

Our journey continues either as a story of pain or a journey of healing.

We move forward whether we like it or not. That's how this life works. The good news is that you'll have many chances to act on the messages you receive. And you can still honor and thank your inner guidance for sending them, while saying you're scared too. Ask your inner guidance to assist you along the way, and you'll likely be amazed at how much you're supported.

After I receive a message, I always say "thank you, thank you, thank you." And if I receive something and I don't feel like I'm ready to act, I'll also say "thank you for sending me this message. Please help me to release any resistance to acting on it," or, "please guide me and show me what the next best step is that's in the highest and greatest good of me and the Universe." Then I remain open to whatever answers and messages I'm given.

This means we have to be unattached to the guidance we're given, to surrender and trust that we are being guided along the way. This can be hard to do, I know. That's why I try to walk through the day being aware of the people I pass, the comments I may overhear, the serendipitous timing of a friend calling and mentioning something that I was just thinking about. When we're open to observing the world around us, and when we pay attention to all the synchronicities, then it helps us stay open to whatever unexpected messages we may receive.

The next time you're out, try to pay attention to your surroundings. Notice if you walk by a feather on the ground, but there are no birds around. That's a message. What were you thinking about when you saw the feather?

How were you feeling? Where were you headed? What had you just finished? These kinds of questions can help train you to be more aware of all the messages you're being sent.

Live your life in awareness and gratitude because gratitude brings joy. Joy brings laughter. It all blends and it's all here to help guide you toward creating a new life that honors your loved one and your Self.

Strengthening Your Connection with Your Loved One

The more you learn to listen and take action on what you hear, the stronger your connection to the Divine becomes. Which means, *your connection to your loved one's spirit grows too.*

Learning to listen and then acting on what we hear, creates a stronger communication channel. I remember one Christmas, many years after Logan's transition, I decided to get a tree and decorate it. I was in a good place in my life, and, while I still missed my boy and felt sadness, I also felt joy and gratitude for my life and all the blessings I had been given. As I was decorating, I felt the pang of missing Logan and wished he were there with me. I asked for a sign from him to let me know he was with me as I decorated.

I needed more hooks for the tree and went to find some. I felt a sudden urge to go open an old trunk that was labeled garland. I didn't think twice about it and was hoping I could find some hooks in there. I just got up, walked into the basement, and opened the trunk. I hadn't opened it in years and when I did, there, sitting on top of the pile, was an old Christmas card that Logan had made me when he was just a little boy. What's even more special about it was the card was dated December 14th, and I had found it on . . . December 14th, fourteen years later! You can't make this stuff up!

I wept and laughed and I felt so blessed that he was

continuing to give me signs that were indisputable that he was still so close to me.

These are the gifts that we're given when we learn to listen and take action on the messages we're sent.

It all connects.

We're not taught any of this. We're not taught about the world of spirit, of Divine guidance and inspiration, or about connecting to our loved ones. While the physical body is no longer here, their spirit is. I've witnessed this every day. Our loved one's energy is still around us.

The more we release the need to control every detail of our lives, the more we're willing to listen to the whispers of our hearts, and willing to act on the inspiration we're given, the more we can connect to this energy and ultimately to our loved one's spirit form.

Our actions in the physical world—signing up for that new class, changing careers, leaving unhealthy relationships, starting new ones, starting a non-profit, moving, going to yoga for the first time, speaking publicly—cement our connection. That's a good thing.

- -

~ DAILY PRACTICE ~

Take one step, a small one, outside your comfort zone in the direction that you're being guided. The options are endless, listen to the messages. Maybe you're being called to start a nonprofit, so maybe you start researching what legal paperwork and advisors you need to gather. Maybe you're being called to change careers, so maybe you sign up for one online class in the new field or you apply for an evening program that moves you toward a new certification or degree? Maybe you're being called to change a relationship, like it's not working with your spouse, so maybe it's talking to them about going to a marriage counselor together, or maybe it's making plans to separate. Maybe you're being called to spend more time in nature or take care of your body and health differently. Maybe you're called to invest more in your healing like trying a different modality or working with a new therapist or healer.

If you're unsure, you can ask for guidance. You can say, "If it's meant to be, please give me a sign or make it easy for me. Drop something or someone in front of me."

Remember what step you take doesn't matter as much as just taking it does.

- -

Chapter 13

Uncover Hidden Wounds

Years before I left my executive position, moved to Charlotte, and began running my private healing practice full-time, there was a moment when I thought about giving up my purpose entirely.

It was about two years after I had begun speaking publicly again and doing intuitive healings, and, for the most part, my life seemed to flow well. On the outside, everything looked great. I had all the external trappings that should have made me happy. I was still working as the executive vice president for the association. I was married, lived in a beautiful home, and drove a nice car. I had my side business as a public speaker, emotional healing coach, and intuitive healer, which was growing as I helped more people heal. I was doing my daily healthy living practices. And I continued to invest in my healing by working with my therapist and seeking out other modalities when I felt I needed them. I was listening to my inner guidance and I felt connected to Logan in spirit form.

I was doing everything that I "should," yet I felt numb,

empty. I was going through the motions in life, and nothing felt right.

There were things I wanted to do that my inner guidance was telling me to, but for some reason, I couldn't take action. I felt blocked, and when I finally mustered the ability to put something into motion, it was *so* hard.

For example, I was on a roll with my public speaking, but then I stopped. I felt like I couldn't do it anymore. It felt too painful being on stage and talking about Logan, and I felt like a fraud, wondering if I had anything worth sharing. I would grow disappointed and disillusioned when only a few people, at most a dozen, would show up to hear me speak. I wanted a packed audience. I would become discouraged after advertising on social media and in local and state newspapers, yet only a handful of people would show up.

If this was my purpose, why are people not showing up? I couldn't understand what was happening.

When I started speaking publicly again, I also thought it would be easier. I never thought speaking about Logan and sharing our story would be easy—even today it's not entirely. But I thought it would be easier. I had spent years healing and working with professionals. I was more accepting of what had happened with Logan, and I felt driven to get out there again and talk to people, helping them heal.

Yet, when I took the stage at a high school or spoke in front of a small group of people, it would bring up so much pain about how my son wasn't here physically, that I began shutting down after each event. I would fall into the darkness again, and that made me feel so frustrated, like I was a failure. How could I talk about healing and staying emotionally healthy and loving life, when, after I delivered those messages, I felt anything but?

This created a lot of self-judgement. "Who do you

think you are?" I would tell myself. "Who do you think you are to speak out on this, standing up there, and teaching anyone when you're not fully healed yet?" "Who do you think you are to stand on that stage? You didn't go to college until you were an adult and now you think you can teach people?"

I didn't want to do the work anymore to build a business that helped others heal, yet I also really did! It was confusing. My inner guidance kept telling me that was the right direction and I needed to do it. I felt that purpose. But then I was riddled with doubts and insecurities about my abilities to follow through.

I had created a website working with a web designer, but it became too complicated. I couldn't find the right words or explain what I was doing, and I didn't have any ideas on the color schemes or layouts. I couldn't answer any questions or give him direction, and so I just didn't do anything with it. I didn't want to deal with it anymore, so I quit half-way through building it.

I was doing intuitive, Tarot and Oracle Card readings for some of my friends, but I didn't take it further than that.

Everywhere I looked in my life, I couldn't get any momentum and I stopped making the progress I wanted. That just compounded my insecurities, and I even started doubting my inner guidance. Maybe this wasn't the direction I was supposed to go?

My healthy morning routine started to slip too. I wasn't meditating or journaling as long. I stopped going for walks outdoors, and I began watching the news more often too. I stopped paying as close attention to my food choices, and I began drinking more frequently.

And while in the last chapter I encouraged you to listen and act on what your inner guidance tells you, I'll admit—I didn't always do this. There were many times that

I resisted. Progress was never linear, but rather it was a step forward, a few back, a couple forward, then I would stall. I lost count of the number of times someone would talk to me about how they wanted a reading from a medium, intuitive, or a Tarot Card reader and my inner voice would say, "Tell them! Tell them you do that and that you would be happy to assist them." But I was so concerned about what people would think of me, that I wouldn't speak up.

I was so frustrated, and I had no idea where to turn or what to do. I knew there was something inside of me that was fighting and resisting. It didn't want me to move forward. I knew my body was holding onto some pattern that told me "stay where you are, you'll be safer. Don't go into the unknown, don't break out of the past, that's dangerous."

Simultaneously, I knew I had to keep consciously moving through my healing journey. That was how I would keep honoring my son and being true to my Self. I just didn't know how to do it because I didn't know what was happening to me or why.

My spark had faded. I was back to just existing, and nothing in my life made me feel happy or content inside. What had I done to mess up my life?

For the first time, I wondered if I needed medication. I didn't want to go on it, but maybe it was time. I fully support the use of medication for many people. I know how truly beneficial and necessary it is for millions, and I would never tell someone to stop taking it. For me, it wasn't something I wanted to use, but I felt so desperate and scared that I talked to Brooke, my therapist, about it.

To my surprise, after much discussion, she suggested that I may have hidden pain and trauma that was separate from Logan's transition that needed healing. She suggested that I do a 12-week intensive treatment designed to address

Post Traumatic Stress (PTS) symptoms. *Hidden pain? Trauma? PTS?* It took me by surprise. Sure, I had been through a lot as a young child and an adult, so her suggestion wasn't outlandish to me, but it was still unexpected.

"If you do this, be prepared, because your life will change," Brooke told me.

I was so desperate to feel good again and to generate momentum helping more people heal through their pain that I was willing to try anything, so I agreed.

I didn't know it at the time, but this would become a major turning point in the direction of my life.

Uncovering Hidden Wounds

Sometimes, we get stuck on our healing journey. We don't know why or how, but what I've found is that often it's connected to some internal pain or wound that needs healing. Sometimes that pain comes from unexpected sources. Logan's transition shattered me in more ways than I realized. It dislodged other traumatic experiences from my past that I had never dealt with, partly because I didn't know I needed to, and because I had no idea how.

My way of dealing with traumatic experiences such as a divorce, a job loss, or even degrading remarks from someone was to ignore whatever happened, to shove it deep inside of me, and never to look at it again. I would use those experiences as fuel to prove to the world that I was as good as anyone else and that I was going to make a difference. I would work even harder and put in longer hours just to excel professionally in the world; taking action more than feeling the feeling.

That was the only way I could keep going forward in my life. In many ways, my past fueled me to give my children a safe and happy home, to have the strength to be a single-mom, to go to college in my forties and earn a degree, to start a business, and to become a lawmaker.

I made it to those places in life because I erected strong walls around my early traumas. I didn't know it at the time, but Logan's transition cracked those walls until eventually that stored pain came pouring out.

One trauma can trigger previous traumas, so, if you suddenly find yourself experiencing flashbacks that you haven't thought about in years, or if you thought you were "over it," please know that you're not alone.

Unresolved trauma can get stored in our bodies for lifetimes. As I began healing more layers of my past, I learned so much about this concept from experts like Dr. Joe Dispenza, an author, researcher, and speaker whose work focuses on helping people rewire their brains and recondition their bodies, so they can change their lives. Dr. Bessel van der Kolk, author of the incredible book, *The Body Keeps The Score*, and Dr. Deborah Sandella with Regenerating Images in Memory (RIM) and author of *Goodbye Hurt and Pain*, also write and speak extensively on this topic.

What they talk about is that sometimes, when we have hidden pain, it can manifest as a feeling of being stuck in our lives. We may know what actions and direction to walk, but we literally can't. Sometimes, we also have no idea what to do, and we can't figure out what's going on, but we know that how we're living and experiencing life is off.

Sometimes our hidden wounds may also show up as excess weight, strange pain in our bodies that no doctor can treat, difficult relationships, or self-sabotaging, repetitive patterns where the same kinds of people or situations keep appearing.

If you find yourself repeating patterns that make you feel bad about yourself, ashamed, worthless, or unlovable, then those could be signs that you have hidden pain that needs your care and attention. This pain may, or may not, be connected to your loved one's transition. If there's pain, it needs releasing, otherwise we may find resistance, and we may not make the progress we know we can on our healing journey. This is an opportunity for you to resolve older wounds and to change the patterns of your past behaviors. When we change the patterns, we release whatever resistance is inside of us, and we're able to move forward, making progress along our journey, creating a more fulfilled life.

There are many ways to clear out the hidden pain. If it is especially traumatic—like physical or sexual abuse, losing a parent or loved one when you were a child, being in a horrific accident—and if you're having PTS symptoms, then you will likely need to work with someone who can help you get into your body to release what you're holding onto.

We're learning that trauma can get stuck in our bodies, and so, to release it, we have to go deep into the body to dissolve and remove it, then we can recreate new patterns. Usually, talk therapy, just thinking positive thoughts, or going to professional development seminars isn't enough to resolve this kind of hidden pain. I've found that I've had to intentionally find healing modalities and work with healers and therapists to move through my emotional blocks, limiting beliefs, and the stored trauma trapped within my body (and soul).

For me, it's taken a combination of healing modalities and therapies.

I started by doing a 12-week intensive therapy program aimed at helping address PTS symptoms that I was having. I didn't realize it was PTS at the time until we started exploring them. Before Logan's transition, I had already lived through quite a few traumatic experiences that I had blocked out. My birth father was an alcoholic who was physically and emotionally abusive. One night he came home so drunk, that he grabbed his gun and started shooting at my mom, my sister, and me. We hid in the bathroom with the door locked. In middle school I was bullied terribly. These were a few of the intense experiences that I lifted the veil on to begin processing and healing.

Working with Brooke helped me immensely but, like everything else, my road to uncovering hidden pain and healing took years. I explored other healing modalities off and on as the years went by. I eventually hired a business coach/energy healer who could help me with accountability on taking action and assisted me with daily energy healing practices. She also taught me how to cut cords with people from my past and present. This process assisted me with ending the energetic ties I had with past relationships that continued to have a hold over me. Energetically cutting these cords could free you from the hold they have over you.

I also did RIM sessions to help me continue releasing my hidden wounds, many that I didn't realize I was carrying. During one of my sessions, I realized I was holding resentment toward my Mom for staying with an abusive man. Through this modality, I was able to become more aware of how brave she was to have stayed. She made that choice because she was afraid her children would be taken away from her. She took the abuse in order to protect my sister and me, until the man, who would become my adopted dad but who I consider to be my father in every way, came into our lives and helped my mom safely leave the marriage.

It was through RIM that I was able to move through and process some of the sexual abuse I experienced as a child too. With RIM, I was able to move through the shame

I had carried from the abuse, and the blame I had placed on myself for what had happened to me. I hadn't realized it, but those experiences had created programs in me which became patterns in my life as an adult. I had unhealthy personal relationships and lived with a constant need to prove myself professionally.

For me, RIM changed my life, and I found such success using that healing modality that I have since gone on to study to be a Master Facilitator—that's how powerful and transformational I've found this practice to be. To give you an example, during one RIM session, I was taken back to my early childhood years when I was 3-year-old to find when and why my limiting beliefs and insecurities were formed.

This was when my father was shooting at my mom, sister, and me. The limiting belief came from how my mom had hidden me between the wall and the toilet, while she had grabbed my sister and the two of them had laid in the bathtub. The program I had originally placed in my head was that I was separate and alone and why wasn't I "loved" enough to be in the tub with my sister and mother? But the reality of the situation was that the only place we all could be safe was for my mom to put me where she did. That was the safest place for me to be, and she made that choice out of unconditional love for me, and her instinct to protect and care for me. I know that now, but the three-year-old in me didn't, and I had grown up with this mistaken belief.

Working with these healers, I also learned about my physical weak spots, those areas in my body where I tend to store and hold pain. Everyone has them. For me, it's my shoulders, neck, and back. It felt almost crippling, that's how intense and strong it was. I had lived with it my entire life, never once questioning or wondering if there was something wrong. I figured that's how my body was—I was so wrong!

Pause for a second and think about your body. Do you have a spot that always acts up or seems aggravated? Maybe it's not a spot; it could be your stomach is always upset or regularly get headaches.

The more I worked with energy healers, the more hidden pain and stored trauma I could release, and I saw clearly unhealthy patterns that I had kept repeating throughout my life. These were patterns in the relationships and partners I chose. I often stayed silent and kept my desires and ideas to myself for fear someone would reject me, or that my voice didn't matter.

As I kept going inward, I faced more feelings of shame and unworthiness and uncovered how much I had believed (mistakenly) that I was unlovable. So many of my choices and actions throughout my life had been about proving myself to others.

As I worked deeper with more healers, I came to understand that I was healing my emotional body and, as I did that, I healed my mind and physical body—and ultimately my soul—too. As I did this, my body felt better, lighter, and my resistance to moving forward with my business, speaking, intuitive readings and healings diminished.

The website started to flow smoother, meaning I'd make a decision based on my inner guidance. Key phrases, descriptions, and words would pop into my mind. People who had key expertise and skills that I was looking for showed up in my life.

More speaking opportunities came my way too. I spoke at a local high school on suicide prevention and how to respond when a friend needs help or has transitioned. I spoke during the statewide Suicide Prevention Awareness day, and the statewide mental health day for physicians and mental health providers. I spoke at major companies and non-profits about suicide prevention in the workplace. I spoke at numerous businesses and organizations after someone had died by suicide, and talked to teams about investing in their healing and how managers and bosses can support their grieving employees.

My life started flowing in an easier, more gentle, and serendipitous way as my inner resistance, frustration, and angst disappeared. I never would have believed any of this was possible or that I had so much unresolved pain.

You have to do the work. You have to be willing to consciously step into that pain one hour at a time. If that sounds scary or exhausting, I understand. You've already done so much work around your loved one's transition. I remember thinking, *more? I have more pain to release? Haven't I been through enough with Logan?*

But I am so glad I chose to work on my hidden pain, because it has allowed me to do the work that I'm being guided to do today. I wouldn't be where I am if I hadn't gone inward to heal the old wounds. I am connected and feel Logan's spirit around me all the time. I have these amazing, loving relationships with the people in my life. I appreciate life fully and feel the expansiveness and appreciation for the gift that we're given in a way that I didn't before I did this intense work.

Plus, I found that, while it was hard sometimes to face the painful memories, I also had more tools and felt more resilient. I remember thinking at one point during the 12-week intensive therapy, *well, I've lived through my son's suicide. I've survived that and I've found a way to keep moving forward in my life. If I can do that, then I can do anything. There is no past experience or pain that can ever compare to Logan's transition, so I can do this.*

I truly felt like I could face whatever was in my past, because I'd already endured so much with Logan's transition.

The same is true for you too. I know that whatever is stored inside of you that's preventing you from moving through your pain and forward in the direction you're being guided, you can release too. I know it's cliché, but I firmly believe that the Divine only gives us what we can handle and are ready for. And I also know it doesn't seem fair to you either. I get that! You've endured a lot already.

Just as working through your loved one's transition will help you release the old, stored pain, the reverse is true too. I reached more inner peace about Logan's transition when I realized that my past painful, traumatic experiences had a higher purpose. They had, in fact, helped me to survive Logan's transition. Those experiences had given me the strength to endure the pain of losing my son, and they taught me resiliency, determination, and survival.

Like just about everything in this book (and life), releasing our hidden pain can take time and patience. Depending on how long you've held onto those traumatic experiences, you may need to work with a specialist or energy healer for multiple sessions over weeks and months.

I found doing an intensive PTS treatment and working with different energy healers and modalities, like RIM, to be extremely effective. These might be options you're drawn to and find success with as well. You may also turn to other treatments too. Maybe you work with a chiropractor, acupuncturist, massage therapist, a trauma-informed yoga instructor, or a shamanic ceremony with or without plant medicine. Find what works for you and embrace that.

I also want to mention that sometimes we never learn or remember where the hidden wound came from. Some people don't want to know either. I did. But many people don't need to know where, why, or how that wound formed. If you don't want to know, or if you can't find it, please know that's okay too. It's normal. You're fine. There is nothing wrong with you. You can still heal those wounds without knowing their origins.

Logan's transition shattered every part of me, and, as I have continued on my healing journey, I've had to pick up every piece, including the ones that I locked away. But I'm so grateful that I have, and, in a way, it feels like Logan has guided me to do this. Releasing my hidden pain and healing those old wounds have freed me and allowed me to serve in a higher capacity assisting others through their healing journey.

If you are struggling with moving forward, or if you feel like you're going through the motions, yet you feel like you're in a good place with your loved one's transition, then consider whether hidden pain may be at the root. If it is, or even if it's your loved one's transition, please love yourself enough to seek more help and guidance.

Your life and your happiness are worth it.

. . . .

~ DAILY PRACTICE ~

I strongly encourage you to work with a professional for this. However, you can begin to do some simple practices at home. One that I find useful is cord cutting. While in a meditative state, you can visualize cords between you and a person, an experience, a place, or a thing that's connected to your hidden pain. If no image comes to mind, imagine your pain and a cord running from you to it. Have a dialog with this image/being and start by saying, "The freedom I'm gaining by cutting this visceral cord . . ." and continue describing your thoughts until you feel complete.

Then, visualize cutting that cord and handing it back to the person, experience, place, or thing on the other end. As you do this, you can repeat "I release you with love and light. I release you with love and light." See, imagine, and experience where the cord was and fill that space with golden white light from the Divine.

. . . .

Chapter 14

Allow Unexpected Grief

Five years after Logan's transition I felt the best that I had since he left the physical world. I had continued releasing hidden pain and was reframing old stories. I had a fairly healthy lifestyle. I was doing my daily morning routines, journaling, spending time in nature, eating healthy. I had my side business as a motivational speaker, emotional healing coach, and was giving intuitive readings for friends of friends.

Life wasn't perfect and I wouldn't say I was healed from Logan's transition, but I was in a good place. At least, that's what I thought.

After Logan's transition, Ashley turned to yoga to help her. She fell in love with the practice and went on to become a teacher and instructor. She was hosting one of her first weekend yoga retreats in the mountains of North Carolina, and I went.

I didn't go for the yoga as much as to support my daughter. What a weekend! She was phenomenal. I had never seen her so poised, confident, yet compassionate and empathetic.

I was awed and inspired to see this young woman transform in front of me, and I felt like such a proud mama bear watching her shine.

I knew Logan's transition had been so hard on her. She and her brother had always been close. They were close in age—just one year, one month, one week, and one day apart—but they had this unusually incredible bond. I saw them as twin flames and best friends. Losing Logan has been so devastating and heart wrenching for her. I know she was doing her best to find her way through her own grief.

Yoga was that salvation and outlet and it became her way of giving back too. I could see how she was using her experience with Logan to extend more healing, grace, kindness, and compassion to all her students. What a gift she was—and still is.

Personally, the weekend astounded me. I thought I had been living a very healthy, balanced lifestyle, but those few days took it to the next level. It was a plant-based-only diet, which I found my body responded so well too. (I've since gone vegan.) We did yoga, went on nature walks, and meditated multiple times each day. I would fall into my bed at night feeling so content and fulfilled in a way that I had never experienced.

Late one afternoon, I found myself in child's pose, my head touching the cool yoga mat, when my mind drifted to Logan. I went from feeling serene and joyful to tears welling in my eyes. They came on so strong. I held my breath trying to choke them down, when I noticed a sharp, hot pain spread across my chest.

It felt like Logan had transitioned all over again, and I lost it. I completely broke down.

It was like a dam had been unleashed, and the water and pain and all this grief spilled everywhere. I was crying over what would never be; that I would never have more moments to see him grow like I was watching Ashley.

That's when I realized: *Dear God, I'm still grieving for the life that is gone and that I'd never have. Will this ever end? Will I ever be at peace?*

Grief Is Not Linear

We live in a society that's built on speed. We expect instant everything. Lose weight, build a business, get in shape, change careers, find our soulmates, achieve success—whatever that means—overnight. From our smart phones to tablets to text messaging, social media, and apps, the speed at which we live life today is turbocharged.

When it comes to grief, at a societal level we tend to expect to wrap that up quickly too. Just look at our workplace policies. Many organizations offer ten days of bereavement for immediate family only. Ten days. That's it, and, when you're back at work, you're expected to perform, be productive, be efficient, and have your "head in the game" as if nothing has changed.

The subliminal message is that it's time to move on and get back to your life.

Well, I call BS!

Everything has changed, and no, ten days isn't enough time to grieve. Ten weeks isn't, ten months isn't, heck ten years may not be, because you don't move on, ever. Yes, you will move through each stage of grief, eventually. But in my experience, grief isn't a linear process, and I didn't move through the five-stages of grief (denial, anger, bargaining, depression, acceptance, and the sixth that David Kessler added, finding meaning) one at a time either.

After Logan's transition, I read so many books, watched so many videos, and talked to so many grief experts because

I needed to learn how to handle these intense emotions. So much of what I read led me to believe we move through each stage one by one, and then I'd be at the end and grief would magically be in my rearview mirror; maybe that is because I wanted to believe that.

But that wasn't my experience. Sometimes I felt so angry and rage-filled, and other times I would get so sad and I couldn't stop crying, but then, as quick as snapping my fingers, the anger and rage would return. My emotions flipped multiple times throughout a day or week.

Grief is intense and it changes over time.

In the very beginning, the grief was constant and I felt it physically in my body. I felt heavy and it hurt to breathe. As I moved through my healing journey, the physical pain subsided, and I felt lighter.

The more pain you release and the more you move through whatever stages of grief arise, the pain does lessen in intensity, and it will hit you less frequently. I like to think of grief as emotional waves instead of stages. An emotion will arise, and we can fight by denying or ignoring it, or we can ride it into the shore. Our emotions will ebb and flow, and once you become aware of what you're feeling in the moment, the easier it will be for you to know what you need to do to help that emotion move through you.

At first I never knew what to do with the intense emotions. Now I do. When grief strikes, when I feel sad and miss Logan's physical presence, I can identify those emotions and will intentionally make choices to support myself in moving through the pain. I can journal and write all my thoughts and feelings. I can go for a quiet walk outside or hike in the mountains. I can call a dear, trusted friend and talk about him. I can head to the ocean and swim or walk on the beach. I can find a quiet space and let myself cry. It can be as easy as finding where I am holding it in my body, allow the feeling by becoming aware of it, and be still with it until it lessons or dissolves.

As I write this book I'm close to the ten-year mark since Logan's transition. Ninety-nine percent of the time, I feel light, joyful, amazing, connected, and so blessed to be alive, so grateful that Logan gifted me with those 19-years together, and incredibly fortunate that I'm moving through this world with my beautiful daughter, and my dear friends and family, and that I still feel intensely connected to him spiritually.

And there are still times when loss and sadness hits unexpectedly. I'm not talking about the holidays or important times of the year that are still hard. I know to expect that if it comes up. But I'm talking about the days when just miss him.

I'm not sure this ever goes away, and I'm not sure I want it to. This is the fullness of life. We do not live in an either (joyful) or (sad) world. We live in both, and to feel the lightness and love around us means we're open to feeling the heaviness of life and grief too. So, I let myself feel whatever comes up, even the grief (although now I feel like it is sadness more so than grief), but it doesn't last as long and it's not as painful as it was before.

No matter how long you've walked this road, just know that whatever you feel, it's okay. If you find yourself hit with grief a year later, it's okay. If it's five years later, that's okay too. If you find yourself feeling a bit sad 10, 20, or 30 or more years after their transition, that's still okay.

Grief isn't linear, it will continue popping up, even in unexpected times.

The key is allowing yourself to move through and experience whatever you're feeling. Give yourself permission to feel all of this without judgement. Continue investing in your healing. Continue using your healthy daily practices and add new ones whenever you need.

The healing journey is truly a journey. We can choose to live a life of pain or we can choose to live a journey of healing. You will be challenged numerous times on this path, but I believe in you. I know that you can learn to move through whatever you're experiencing. And don't let anyone tell you how to grieve—not even me! This is your journey. Give yourself the permission to travel your unique path through, and to, healing.

. . . .

~DAILY PRACTICE ~

Give yourself permission to feel whatever you're feeling and to move through it. Pick one activity like journaling, going for a hike, taking a hot bath, crying, and let the emotion flow through you instead of blocking or ignoring it. If you can, give yourself as long as you need to let the emotion flow through you. That could be as little as five minutes or as long as 20-30, maybe even more.

Allowing yourself to feel what you feel in real-time is important, but I also know that sometimes we're not in the right place, like if we're at work. If that's the case, try and give yourself at least a little space to compose yourself, maybe head to the restroom and wash your hands, or splash your face, or take five to ten-minute break outside.

Then, as soon as you're in a place where you can work through those emotions in a healthy and safe area, then do it. That may mean you wait until you're home from work or after the kids are in bed. The sooner you can allow yourself the space to let those emotions flow through you, the easier it will be for them to move and you'll reduce the chances that they become lodged—and forgotten—inside your body. Schedule time for you to move through your emotions. There is no judgement on how you do it. It is your process and you have a responsibility to yourself to feel what you feel, and to move through it in a way that's healthy and safe for you.

You are meant to live a free and fulfilled life.

. . . .

Chapter 15

Be Gentle with Yourself

About eight years after Logan's transition, my life changed pretty dramatically again, although this time from decisions I intentionally made. I finalized my divorce, left my full-time job, moved from Vermont, where I was born, raised and had lived my entire life, and relocated to Charlotte, North Carolina to be closer to my daughter, *and* I went all-in on growing my private-practice and small business.

I did all of that within nine months.

I had only been living in Charlotte for a few weeks before I put together an ambitious schedule and plan for what I expected to have accomplished within twelve months.

I planned to:

- Write this book
- Create online classes
- Schedule multiple speaking events
- Triple my client list
- Become a certified RIM facilitator (which

included attending multiple in-person, week-long training sessions in Colorado)

- Hold bi-weekly, in-person energy healing and oracle card readings at a local business in Charlotte

- Continue my own personal development and ongoing healing

- Commit to daily workouts; and

- Develop new personal relationships in my new hometown.

Just seeing this list makes me laugh. What was I thinking?!

It will probably come as no surprise that I didn't come close to achieving this list. Many of the items I moved in the right direction, but overall, my accomplishments were modest, and I took more breaks and had to slow down my pace more than I had anticipated. Often, I didn't choose to slow down; I was forced to. I kept getting sick—I even broke out in shingles. External delays hit me. Writing the book and creating online courses turned out more difficult than I had expected.

Yet, for every delay or time I was forced to slow down, I found myself grateful for it because I needed the rest. My mind, my body, my heart, my soul needed the break, and I had to learn how to find a more reasonable and sustainable pace.

Once I figured out that breaks were good, and it was okay to hit the pause button occasionally, I discovered that when I was ready to move forward again, I did it with more energy and focus. That made the projects flow smoother and I didn't struggle as much.

Be Gentle with Yourself

Surviving your loved one's transition is one of, if not the single, most challenging experience you may ever go through in your life. And you're doing it. You are surviving and you will thrive. Maybe you've already felt glimpses of this, and maybe not. You have come so far already in this book, so congratulations!

And do you ever feel so exhausted you just want a break from the intensity, from the pain, from the need to move forward in recreating a new life and honoring your loved one's legacy?

I know I do!

At times it's grueling. Don't get me wrong, the journey that Logan's transition thrust me on has showed me how much love I have to give and receive. It's completely changed my life in miraculous ways. I have such a deep connection with my daughter, Logan, my mother, and my father. I have incredible friends, new ones and old, who have stood by me, listening, loving, and supporting me. I feel the healthiest in my body, mind, heart, and soul that I ever have. I love my work as a certified success coach, an energy healer, global speaker, author, and certified RIM facilitator.

I feel blessed every day for the connection I have with my inner guidance, to the Divine, and to Logan in spirit form. I hold so much gratitude and thanks for my son who has helped me every step of the way.

There have been so many amazing moments, but also some really difficult ones too. Intense grief and frustration, anger and fear have appeared in my life again and again. I've faced setbacks and unexpected delays, like when I was trying to make progress with my business and work as a healer and I felt blocked, or when unexpected grief struck.

Here's what I've learned: we do the best we can with what we have in each moment. And, I dare say, that each layer of grief, setback, or block I experienced I now can look back on and see why it happened.

Our healing journeys are filled with starts and stops. We'll see a therapist or an energy healer for a period of time, and then we'll let it go for some time, and then we'll return to experience a different healing modality or even another therapist. We'll move forward and make progress in whatever direction we're being guided and we'll want to stop. We'll hit the pause button, because we need a break, a chance to catch our breaths, or we'll be forced to halt as everything in life just feels hard, like we're pushing and pushing and pushing against the Universe to make any progress.

When (not if) you hit these moments, please be gentle and kind with yourself. It's alright to take breaks to pause and catch your breath. Your healing journey is not a race. It's not a sprint. And there's no finish line you have to meet.

Learning how to care for yourself in each moment is one of the most important gifts you can give to yourself and, I might say, the Universe. In North Carolina, I couldn't ignore how hard I was pushing. I had to step back, slow down, and look behind me at everything I had created and how far I'd traveled since Logan's transition. Creating a new life that honors you and your loved one, that's aligned with your true and authentic Self now, is a journey in and of itself.

There will be moments when you need to pause to honor and celebrate the road you've traveled so far. Do that.

I want you to know that I've paused my healing journey so many times. That doesn't always come through in a book. I have to simplify my story in some ways and mark the major milestones, so it's hard to see that I've circled around to many of the lessons in this book numerous times in the last ten years. I'm probably on my third or fourth go-around by now.

So, wherever you are on your healing journey, please be gentle with yourself. If you need to pause, do it. If you need to return to working with a healer or professional therapist, do it. If you need to double-down on living your purpose, do it. Give yourself what you need, whatever that may be.

If that's hard to do right now, if it's difficult to grant yourself permission, then let me do it for you. I will celebrate you right now, because I see you. I see how hard you've worked to get to this place. I'm really proud of you for making it this far. And I'll grant you permission to give yourself whatever you need. You deserve it and you're worth it.

You are exactly where you are supposed to be on your journey in this exact moment.

. . . .

~ DAILY PRACTICE ~

Pause. Breathe. Reflect on how far you've traveled already. Celebrate your wins by writing down all the steps you have already taken. Review it, read it aloud. Feel proud of that. You are doing such a tremendous job. Go easy on yourself. Be gentle and kind and give yourself whatever you need in this moment. If it's a bubble bath, do it. If it's playing a round of golf, do it. If it's biking, hiking, walking, do it. If it's making a cup of tea and curling up with a book, do it. If it's gardening, calling an old friend, playing with your dog, taking a yoga class, baking . . . whatever you need, please give yourself that. Slow down and focus on what you need. Be with yourself.

. . . .

Chapter 16

Forgive Yourself

I'm a huge believer in ongoing learning and personal and professional development. For me, it's closely connected to investing in my healing. I'm committed to both and I've found that each feeds the other. Without the healing, the personal development would have been for nothing as I wouldn't have done much with it. And without the skills I have gained through personal development, I would have only kept my healing to myself.

For weeks I kept seeing an ad on my social media feed about a professional development seminar in Boston, led by Jack Canfield, co-author of the successful *Chicken Soup for the Soul* books. At first, I ignored the pull to go, but then, after seeing it for the fifth time, I actually opened the ad and looked closer.

I wanted to hone my public speaking skills and stage presence, and I could feel my inner guidance encouraging me to go. Something about the day-long seminar felt so right to me, so I signed up with a friend and, a few weeks later, we found ourselves in a hotel in downtown Boston.

As soon as I walked in the seminar room, I knew I was in the right place. When we broke for lunch, Jack happened to join my table for our meal, and he sat next to me. He asked us all what brought us to the conference and, when it was my turn, I told him and our table an abbreviated story about my work, my mission, and Logan's transition.

Jack looked at me thoughtfully and said that I may want to consider working with him in another program called, "Train the Trainer Live." It was a yearlong commitment, with two week-long, in-person engagements spent in California. He had one spot open, the first live meeting was in three weeks, and suggested that I seriously consider it, then he gave me the name of a staff member to follow-up with for more details, and he wished me luck with whatever I chose.

It was a big commitment, but again I felt that nudge that this was the right choice for me, even though I wasn't sure why. I even did a muscle test, which in kinesiology is a way to use our bodies to determine what is in our best interest using a yes/no response. I had a friend stand with me and watch me to make sure that signing up was the right choice. I got a clear yes from my body, so I signed up and three weeks later I found myself in California, enrolled in Jack's program.

It was one of the best experiences of my life.

Toward the end of our last week-long session, Jack had us do an exercise that began by writing everything that you're hiding. There were several steps after that, and eventually he had us pair up with someone we hadn't worked with that week, and we shared with our partner what we wrote. Then Jack asked if anyone wanted to come on stage and share with the group what they had released through the process of sharing.

A few hands hesitantly went up. I listened in awe and

empathy as I heard people show such vulnerability by standing in front of 120 people and share their deepest, darkest secrets. One woman in particular was incredible, and I thought, *Wow! If she can get up and tell this story, then maybe I can too.*

I half raised my hand, and Jack called on me. I stood on wobbly legs and wanted to back out as soon as I started up the stairs to the stage. I felt nauseous as I looked out and saw everyone staring at me, waiting for me to speak. I took the mic, barely able to hold onto it. With my hands shaking, I took a deep breath, closed my eyes for a second and then I began.

"On the day my son took his life, he left a note and in it he said that he didn't want me to attend his service," my voice trembled as I continued, "When he died, he wasn't speaking to me. He was so angry at me . . ." As tears streamed down my face, I paused to collect myself before revealing something I had never told anyone, not even my closest friends.

I then told the group that I hadn't wanted to get pregnant with Logan.

It had happened so quickly after Ashley had been born that terror set in. How could I raise two children only 13-months apart with a crumbling marriage? My husband and I weren't in a good place, and I wasn't sure we were going to work. I had always wanted my children to know a happy and secure childhood, and that didn't feel like the direction my husband and I were headed. I didn't know what world or what kind of life I would bring a baby into. The last thing I wanted was to bring them into a world of heartache, pain, and struggle, and that's what I feared I would give to them.

Then I miscarried, and I felt ashamed because I had felt relieved.

When I went to the doctor's office to confirm the miscarriage, I was surprised to learn that I was, in fact, *still pregnant*. I had been carrying twins, which I didn't know until I had miscarried one of them.

I felt apprehensive as I carried Logan to term, still unsure what Logan would find in this world. What he found was struggle. He came into this world with his cord wrapped around his neck, twice. Doctors had to quickly work to save him. As an infant, he was always upset and projectile vomited constantly. As a toddler and young child, he had extreme mood swings, tantrums, and outbursts. At the time, I never thought twice about any of this. Looking back, I can see that his life was a roller coaster of struggle.

I shared all of this with the group, and I told them how I blamed myself for his death.

"Did I create this with my thoughts and feelings when I was pregnant with him? Did I cause my son to have a hard life? Did I make the wrong decisions and choices with him? What if I had done things differently, what if I had said or made different choices, would he still be here with me?" I asked. I choked back tears as I revealed my deepest pain, the part of myself that I had never spoken aloud to anyone.

As I admitted everything, I could feel the self-blame and shame rising within in me. I stood on that stage, hating myself for having caused my son's transition.

I was shaking and crying by the time I fell silent. No one said anything as I stood trembling. I looked over at Jack and he held my gaze. He didn't say anything at first, but then he very calmly, quietly, yet firmly asked me, "Did you love him when he was born?"

"Of course, I did," I blurted instinctively.

I kind of smiled as I wiped away the tears and kept talking. "I loved him when he was in my belly, even though I was scared to bring him into this world. I couldn't wait to meet him, and when I did, I just fell in love with him even more." I told Jack and the group how Logan had always seemed the happiest and most content when he was in my arms. I'd hold him when he couldn't sleep, and he'd rest his head on my chest, wrap his little fingers around mine, and finally he'd drift off peacefully—I loved him every second.

Jack smiled at me and, for the first time since I stood on that stage, I smiled too.

Forgiving Ourselves

So much of our healing journey happens in layers. As we keep investing in ourselves, working through our grief and pain and recreating a new life, we go deeper within ourselves where we can reach the experiences, the thoughts, the emotions, the hidden trauma, and the beliefs that are the most painful.

This isn't the same kind of hidden pain we talked about in chapter 13. This is the root of so much of our pain when we lose someone we love suddenly and unexpectedly.

It's the "What if . . ." questions that torment us.

It's the self-blame, self-shame, and guilt we feel surrounding our loved one's transitions. It's all the regrets we have whether it's what we did or didn't say, did or didn't do, and the choices and decisions we did or didn't make.

Everyone whom I have met and worked with has tortured themselves with thoughts like *what if I had done this differently? What if I had said this instead? What if I had acted or spoken up sooner? Maybe if I had done or said something different, then maybe they'd still be here. Maybe I could have changed the course of our future.*

But here's a truth, and it's hard to accept: we had no control over our loved ones, the decisions they made or didn't make, the choices they made or didn't make, and we had no more control over their transition than our parents, friends, or loved ones have over us.

No matter the circumstances, let me repeat, *you had no control over the experience or the choices they made.*

I'm not just talking about loved ones who transitioned from suicide or a drug overdose. This is for anyone who has lost someone suddenly and unexpectedly, whether that's from a car accident, a boating or swimming accident, a robbery gone wrong, a heart attack, a fire, a murder, a health-related experience, a natural disaster, or any other event that you could never have imagined or expected.

I know in the New Age movement there is a lot of focus on manifesting our lives and the Law of Attraction, but please hear me when I say, there are so many circumstances far outside our control that no amount of positive thinking, Law of Attraction, or manifesting our dreams can ever direct. As scary as it is to admit, we are not in as much control as we like to think or believe we are. This is life and there are so many experiences that happen to us that we would never consciously choose—our loved one's transition being just one of them.

How your loved one transitioned, or whatever happened between you and them before they left the physical world, know this: you made the best decisions you could in each moment with what you knew. In my heart, I know and have come to believe this, because I've seen it in the countless people I've worked with. Whatever you said or did, whatever decisions you made or didn't make, all of them came from a place of deep, unending love for your loved one.

Still, I know how hard it is for us to realize this. It's so easy to judge, doubt, and second-guess ourselves. If you're struggling with guilt, shame, or blame and you're finding it hard to forgive yourself—for whatever you feel you did or didn't do, say or didn't say—then please ask yourself these questions:

Did you love them?

Did you do what you thought was best for them with what you knew in every moment?

If the roles were reversed and your loved one was still here, but you had transitioned, would you want them to beat themselves up? Would you want them to live in guilt, shame, blame and self-doubt?

We cannot undo what has happened, and we will always want our loved ones back. I still wish Logan could be here with me and Ashley, and there are still days I second-guess and play the terrible, torturous "what if . . ." game with myself. Even working on this chapter, it took me days to remind myself that Logan had felt the love I had for him every time I caressed my belly when he moved, every time he fell asleep in my arms and wrapped his sweet fingers around mine, every time I would hold him and support him throughout his life.

When I fall back into the "what if . . ." it leaves me feeling down, dark, and depressed. It creates a feeling within me that doesn't resonate with the way I know Logan would want me to feel or the way I want to live my life today. Feeling guilt for my son's transition serves no one. It has no purpose other than to keep me locked in a prison of my own making, and if I allowed myself to stay there, trapped, then I wouldn't be able to do the work I'm doing—speaking out about healing, helping other people to release their pain and heal their hearts, minds, bodies, and souls. I wouldn't honor my son either.

It's easy to fall back into the self-blame game. Just remember, you did the best you could with what you knew at the time.

There is so much goodness, light, love, and peace for you to experience and to give to the world. From the bottom of my heart, I believe each of us has a purpose on this planet, and it's to bring more love, compassion, patience, and peace to the world. Those of us who have experienced the sudden unexpected loss of our loved one, have learned secrets about this world, about loving and letting go, about acceptance and authenticity, about patience and peace, and so much more.

You have gifts and wisdom that this experience will have taught you, but you will not be able to fully embrace and share it if you're trapped in the pain of blame, guilt, and shame.

I invite you to stand with me and forgive yourself. To have grace with yourself. To know and believe in your heart that you did everything that you could with what you knew. You did your best. You loved fully, and you deserve to be free.

I remember being so frightened, believing that so many people were judging me for how I parented Logan and what I did or didn't do. When I stood on that stage at Jack Canfield's training, I was terrified that people I didn't know would judge me for what I was about to tell them.

But guess what? They didn't. I stood in front of all those people, shared my story, and if anything, they embraced me more. They had more compassion for me and what I had been through. As I listened to other people share their stories, I realized that we all have a story. We all have something we're hiding, that we're judging ourselves about. When we judge ourselves, we can't forgive ourselves, we can't let go of the pain or the torture.

The meaning of the exercise that we went through was to open our eyes to the fact that we all are hiding something. If we are willing to share what lives in the dark, then we will find more people who have experienced something similar. Why not be open, vulnerable, and authentic, so you can release the shackles you have chained yourself to for so many years? When we judge ourselves, we're judging other people too, and that creates painful relationships.

I don't want to live in a world where people constantly judge each other. Do you? I want you to know that whatever you're holding onto and judging yourself for, you're not alone. Isn't it time for all of us to lay down our shame, guilt, and blame? Isn't it time for us to be kinder and more forgiving of ourselves?

After I shared my story on that stage, I spent many mornings and nights reflecting on it in meditation and in my journal. I came to realize, not just intellectually but I felt it in my heart, that every choice I had made, every action I had taken, everything I had said to Logan was because I loved him so much and wanted him to be safe, cared for, healthy, and happy. Yes, our last two years were trying, and yes, there are things that I would have done differently, knowing what I know now. I've learned so much about health, emotional fitness, energetic health, moving through emotions, trapped trauma in our bodies, and so much more, that I wish I could have had that wisdom when Logan was alive.

Still, every decision I made was with his best interests in mind. I know I did the best I could with what I knew, and that's all any of us can do.

I said it earlier and I'll say it again, our loved ones don't want us to suffer. This experience that we've endured, they want us to use it as a catalyst to bring more healing, more hope, more inspiration, and more love into the world. That starts with you.

What pearl can you find within this experience? How can you move through your pain to live in your best and highest life? Even after so much pain, how can you serve and give back to your family, friends, and community?

How can you live reflecting your loved one's legacy and honoring who they were? How can you live in peace and love?

The path to peace is forgiveness—forgiveness of yourself.

The more you do the work in this book, the more you can access that forgiveness. When you do, you will find grace for everyone in your life, including you. This is living from your heart, respecting, loving, and caring for you. That ripples throughout the world affecting everyone you meet.

When you forgive yourself, you release yourself from whatever prison that has held you. It frees you to have a more loving relationship with yourself, and with everyone in your life. You will stop judging and instead extend understanding and compassion to them.

To forgive yourself, you have to be willing to look at the experiences you've hidden from your awareness. You have to be willing to acknowledge the shame, blame, and guilt that you're holding.

When you do, when you forgive yourself, then you actually take control over the one part of your life that you have full reign over: your response. We may not control life, but we do control how we respond to experiences, events, people, and our thoughts and emotions.

No, we could not control our loved one's transition, but we do control how we respond to it and what we do with our lives going forward.

Sometimes we don't realize we're carrying this blame, shame, or guilt until we start working through our pain and grief. When we get to this deep inner layer, and we begin resolving and dissolving it, then we open ourselves to other memories. We can remember all the times we cared for our loved ones, how much we showed them that love, and how we stood by them.

We create a new perspective this way and that creates and becomes a positive feedback loop, helping us to continue releasing that inner shame, blame, and guilt while accessing more of the positive, light-filled moments with our loved ones.

Forgiving Others

I'm not proud of this, but I believe in transparency. After our loved one's transition, we experience intense emotions. Blame is one of those. In my case, I blamed people that were close to him like my parents, other family members, and some of his friends whom I saw as enabling his behavior that I saw as harming him and impacting his decisions.

But this was just a story I had created. One that wasn't true.

I realized this as I began releasing my other hidden pain. Logan's transition was no one's fault. Not mine, my parent's, or anyone's. Everyone loved him so, so much. They did the best they could in a terribly challenging and difficult situation. Everyone made the best decisions and choices they could in the moment out of their endless, unconditional love for him.

It was time for me to move through the old story, the one that was filled with anger, pain, resentment, and blame. I had to forgive everyone in Logan's life whom I thought played a role in his suicide.

Judging others is not my job in this life. My job is to pay attention to my actions and responses. It's to own my thoughts and emotions. I wanted my parents back in my life. I wanted to reconnect with my mother and father, who I know have always made choices out of caring and protecting their family—that includes me and all their grandchildren.

The story I had told myself was filled with anger and resentment, and it was just poisoning me and destroying my relationship with people like my parents who were really important to me. When I realized that everyone, including my parents, made every choice concerning Logan from a place of unconditional love and support for him, then how could I hold onto resentment and anger?

Forgiving Your Loved One

I can't talk about forgiveness without also mentioning forgiving our loved ones too.

When we experience a sudden and unexpected loss, other people in our lives may be really angry at our loved one. I had a dear friend who was mad at Logan for taking his life. She saw the devastation and pain that was left and how it deeply affected me, Ashley, and everyone close to him. My friend felt protective toward us.

Other times, it may be that we are the ones who feel angry at our loved ones who died by suicide, a drug overdose, or an accident that we believe could have been prevented. We may feel angry that our loved one didn't get the help they needed, or they couldn't accept help from their families and friends. We may feel upset that our loved one has "left us alone in this world." And we may even be mad at them for what we perceive to have been a bad decision they made, which could have led to an overdose, suicide, illness, or accident.

There are so many situations that can bring out anger toward our loved ones. Please know, if someone you're close with is angry at your loved one, or even if you are, these are normal reactions. When someone transitions suddenly and unexpectedly it ripples throughout so many more people than any of us can realize.

First, try to be kind to anyone in your life who may be angry at your loved one. I remember how, at first, I felt very protective of Logan. I couldn't believe that my friend would be angry at my son. Then, one afternoon I went for a hike in the woods and, as I walked, I realized that my friend was hurting too. There was nothing to "protect" Logan from; this was her experience of his transition and I had to honor what she was going through without judgment. I clearly saw how my friend was actually being very protective of me and Ashley. It hurt her to see us going through what we did. This was a huge awakening for me, and I instantly felt more empathy and compassion toward her and also gratitude to her for being a good friend.

Second, accept whatever reaction you're having and be willing to work through it.

Logan was the last person I felt anger toward. I really blamed myself and everyone around him. There were a few moments when I was upset at him, but for me, it was more about "how could he not feel how much everyone loved him? How could he not realize how much his transition would hurt everyone that he loved and cared for?"

As I worked through those feelings and confusion, I was able to realize that he was in so much pain that he couldn't feel anything else. With suicides and drug overdoses, our loved ones can't feel or see the light. They aren't feeling that Divine connection or hearing their inner guidance because they have a lot of pain.

Often, their decision-making abilities are comprised. Many suicide survivors, for example, talk about how they felt like they were a burden to their families and society, that's why they tried to take their lives. They felt they would do the world a favor.

Like everything we've covered so far in the book, feeling

anger toward our loved ones can be complicated, and like everything else, I encourage you to use whatever healing modality you need to help work through these emotions in a healthy and safe manner.

~ DAILY PRACTICE ~

Forgiveness can take time. It doesn't happen over-night, so be gentle and patient with yourself. One practice that has helped me tremendously has been the Mirror Exercise.

I encourage you to stand in front of a mirror, and, while looking yourself in the eyes repeat out loud "I forgive you. I love you. I forgive you. I love you. I forgive you. I love you."

Repeat this at least three times, or more, until you feel a little relief. At first, it may feel uncomfortable. It did for me. But do this every morning and every night and you will slowly retrain your brain to see yourself with love, appreciation, and gratitude.

And, if you aren't comfortable with looking at yourself in the mirror quite yet, you can also try a Hawaiian prayer called the Ho'oponopono that represents repentance, forgiveness, gratitude, and love. Find a quiet place, close your eyes and breathe in and out a couple of times, so you drop into your heart. Find in your body where you holding the blame or feelings you can't forgive. Then to the energy you have located say, "I'm sorry. I love you. Please forgive me. Thank you." You can say that as many times as you feel the need to until you feel the energy decrease. Feel the forgiveness flow through you as you are saying it. Mean it. Do this until you feel it has dissipated or until it is manageable and then practice it as many times as you need to.

Chapter 17

You Choose

I would never have chosen to go through this experience; I don't think anyone who has lost a loved one suddenly and unexpectedly ever would. For those of us who have, it irrevocably changes us, but how? Will it change us for the better or the worst? Will we lose faith, hope, and light in life? Will it teach us to appreciate how precious this world and all lives in it, including our own, are? Will it trap us in pain, anger, and hatred?

There is no redo, no going back to change what happened. Our loved ones have transitioned. We're left answering this: What will we do with our lives now? How will we live from this moment on?

Finding your way forward will most likely be one of, if not the hardest thing you'll ever do. And while the sudden and unexpected loss is traumatic, and you will continue to miss their presence in the physical world, they have left you gifts as well.

For the first time in my life, I live authentically. I am connected to my inner Self in a way I never was. I know myself better than I ever have. I feel real joy today, more inner peace, and I am fulfilled with my work, my friends and family, and my life.

I appreciate and feel gratitude in a way I never did before. I took everything before Logan's transition for granted. Logan has gifted me this. He has shown me how precious life and this world is, and he's taught me how to help others heal and find more inner peace too.

Although Logan may be gone physically, I still sense his presence with me every day. I know he guides me, and I know that by sharing our story and what he went through, he is helping others to heal too.

The pain you feel around your loved one's transition is real, so what will you do with it? Will you bury or mask it, or will you choose to move through it?

This is the decision you have to make.

Choosing to go on this healing journey, to move through your pain, will transform your life in ways you cannot imagine. Yes, at times it will be painful. Yes, at times you'll probably say, "F**k this. I'm done."

But if you can keep coming back to choosing the healing path, then I know you will find the light within. You will find your inner guidance. You will find how to honor your loved one by living your life fully, wholly, and filled with more love and light.

Without a doubt or hesitation, I would give my life today to have my son's physical presence walk this earth. But that's not mine to choose. Instead, I choose to see the nineteen years I had with him as one of the two greatest gifts I've been given—the second being my beautiful daughter.

I can hold multiple emotions at once. I can feel appreciation for his life; sadness at times that he is no longer in physical form; and joy and gratitude that his transition has taught me how to live and love more deeply, more passionately, more connected, and more gracefully.

Every day, I recommit to honoring him and his spirit—which I know is with me still. Every day, I wake up and do the work to help more people heal, I honor his journey and life purpose. I know mine is directly connected to helping others heal through their pain and suffering after losing a loved one suddenly and unexpectedly.

There is light at the end of your tunnel. There is love, and patience, and inner peace. When you invest in your Self, when you invest in your healing, when you listen to your inner guidance and take steps outside your comfort zone, you begin to pick up the pieces of your shattered life. You will put those pieces back together again. What you create will not look the same as before, and that's okay.

It will be different. It will feel different. It will look different. Because you are different.

That doesn't mean it's bad or good. It's your new reality, and how you choose to move through this life is up to you.

I have chosen the healing journey, and it has made all the difference in the world.

Wherever you are on this journey, whatever path you choose to take, may you find peace, love, and a deeper connection to the world, your Self, and your loved one. Take your journey one hour at a time. Create a healing journey, not a story of pain.

You deserve it.

Gratitude

There are so many incredible people who helped me realize this book.

First, I wouldn't be here if it wasn't for the many amazing people who carried me when I didn't think I could survive. Bianca, Beth, Danielle, Paul . . . and everyone else who stayed by my side when my life shattered, I am forever grateful and thankful to you.

A special thank you to Amanda Ibey, my collaborative writer and dear friend. This book would never have been written if it wasn't for you. I am so grateful that you shared your listening, curiosity, and amazing writing gifts with me. You have been patient, held space for me, and nudged me when I needed it. Before we started this project, I knew deep in my soul that you were supposed to be my writing partner, and I am so thankful to have had you by my side on this journey.

To Kate Butler and her team for helping me design and publish this book. It has been the best working with you. To Jeanne, Danielle, Bianca, Beth, Debbie, John, Donna, Michael, Dr. Deb, Macy, Chris, Jack, Patty, and everyone who read early drafts, made suggestions on the book, and listened as I cried during this process.

Thank you to all the extraordinary teachers whom I have studied with, who have pushed me and sat with me as I shed so much pain along the way. To Jack Canfield and Dr. Deborah Sandella, two gifted healers and teachers whom I am proud to have learned from. I am eternally grateful to Brooke White, who helped get me through the initial stages of grief. Thank you to all my co-workers, colleagues, and friends who have stayed by my side, supporting, encouraging, and loving me throughout this journey.

To my parents, thank you Mom and Dad for raising me, and loving me and my children.

My dearest Ashley, I am so grateful to you for holding on, for not giving up when it would have been easier to. Thank you for being the caring, compassionate, dedicated, strong, and committed daughter that you are. I am beyond grateful to continue walking this journey with you, and I am so proud of the young woman you have become. I love you with all my heart, and I know this book would never have been possible if it wasn't for you.

Thank you, Logan. Thank you for gifting us with those nineteen years, and for providing me with more since you have transitioned. I am so grateful for all the signs you have given me, especially since I started writing this book. I know you have guided me along the way, waking me up to share the cover design and so much more. I love you so much and am so thankful you are my partner in assisting others on their journeys.

I thank and acknowledge all of my guides, the Divine, and all those who came before me.

Finally, I thank you, my reader, for picking up this book and stepping into your healing journey. It's because of you that I wrote this book.

About the Author

CATHLEEN ELLE is a Transformational Speaker, Certified Intuitive Success Coach and Healer, #1 International bestselling author, and co-host of the Podcast: Beyond Your Best Plan. Cathleen has coped with multiple traumas, but the death of her 19-year-old son from suicide was the catalyst that changed her life forever. Today, she's on a mission to help people who have experienced sudden unexpected loss, or who have hidden trauma, to reconnect with their joy, move beyond limiting beliefs, and change the trajectory of their lives. In her work, Cathleen teaches powerful healing techniques to help people move through their traumas. Whether it's a divorce, a job, substance abuse, emotional or physical abuse, illness, or the sudden death of a loved one, Cathleen shows people, in the midst of their healing journeys, how to take the next step by redesigning their lives.

Made in USA - North Chelmsford, MA
1177372_9781952725180
11.02.2021 1343